An introduction to

Propositional Logic
and
Set Theory
2nd Edition

César R.
Gallo P.

Table of Contents

Preface

Mathematics has always been regarded as a difficult subject by most students of any age. It is a common belief that accessing mathematical knowledge requires special skills. Nothing is further from reality. What happens is that the more this false belief spreads, the more it tends to be accepted as a fact. It is not special skills that are required to access mathematical knowledge, but the willingness and desire to learn it. Everyone can succeed in learning mathematics. Once students learn to reason logically, the rest of the knowledge flows easily. In this way, students discover that the process of learning mathematics can be even fun, and they will want to learn more. Consequently, to achieve this goal teaching must begin by familiarizing students with propositional logic. In other words, students must be taught to think logically since mathematics is a logical science. This explains why the beginning of this book focuses on introducing students to this topic.

This book is especially useful for students who are about to finish high school and want to properly prepare in mathematics to start college or university. The book is also suitable for those students who have already started higher education. Many of them still face barriers in learning more complex mathematical concepts and their adequate application. A flaw in understanding basic concepts is what makes them reluctant to learn more. Since the objective is to help students achieve an adequate understanding of basic concepts, this book was written in plain language to make the process of acquiring mathematical knowledge a friendly, enjoyable, and accessible one even for those students who dislike mathematics.

The simplicity of language does not sacrifice the rigor or depth of the study offered in the next pages, which guarantees adequate management of concepts. Students are not required to have math skills; the only requirement is to be interested in learning.

In the three chapters that make up this text, we address the building blocks of Calculus or Mathematical Analysis. We start with Propositional Logic, which provides the language, logical reasoning, and training on how to properly address mathematical proofs. This chapter is followed by an introduction to Set Theory where we develop a body of concepts that are used in the definition of many fundamental concepts of Calculus such as Function. This book ends with the study of the real number system which is addressed from an axiomatic approach.

Throughout the book, we offer examples to illustrate all the concepts that we discuss. Additionally, we propose several sets of exercises to be solved by students. The answers to those exercises are offered at the end of each chapter. Thus, students can check their progress in learning the concepts discussed. The level of difficulty of such exercises varies from the most elementary level to a moderate level since the main objective of this book is to help students to properly learn these basic concepts and not to test their mathematical skills.

Once the students have completed the study of all the concepts discussed in this book, they will be able to approach with a solid base, and with confidence, the study of the concepts of Calculus such as functions, limits, continuity, derivatives, and integrals, which will be discussed in upcoming books by the author.

César R. Gallo P.

Chapter 1: Propositional Logic

Logic is the science that studies form, structures, or schemes of formal reasoning. It establishes the fundamental principles and provides methods to determine what makes certain reasoning valid or not. Propositional Logic deals specifically with propositions, to which this chapter is devoted.

Any language is characterized by being a set of symbols with a certain meaning that we use to establish a certain type of communication. Based on a previous organization, we can build through these symbols (words, signs, musical notes, etc.) certain types of expressions (sentences, operations, musical phrases, etc.). In some cases, ordinary language can be translated into the symbolic language just as some symbolic expressions can be simplified or given some meaning in ordinary language.

Propositional logic is interested only in those expressions that we call propositions, which constitute its basic object.

DEFINITION OF PROPOSITION

> A proposition is a statement or sentence that can be *unequivocally* verified as *true* or *false.*

According to this definition, propositions are declarative expressions that affirm something, for which there is some criterion that allows establishing, without a doubt, if such affirmation is true or false. These values (true or false) are called the *truth values* of propositions.

Examples

a) 17 is an odd number.
b) Shakespeare was born in Japan.
c) What time is it?
d) Damn it!

Expressions *a)* and *b)* are propositions since they can be verified as true or false. In the case of *a)* the definition of what is an odd number is available while in the case of *b)* there is historical information about the birthplace of Shakespeare. In contrast, expressions *c)* and *d)* are not propositions since they are a question and an exclamation respectively that affirm nothing so that they cannot be verified as true or false.

The existence of an explicit, clear, and well-defined criterion to determine unequivocally the truth values is fundamental because the truth or falsity of some affirmations is relative. Depending on the context, the time in which the affirmations are made, and the criterion used, the same expression may be true in some cases and false in others. The following example helps to clarify this.

Let us have the statement: "North Korea is a developed country". To know if this statement is true or false, we first need to establish what it is understood by "developed country". There is a long and unfinished debate about development. Many variables intervene in the discussion which makes it difficult to achieve a unique definition. Therefore, some people will regard that statement as true while others would say it is false. On the contrary when there is a unification of criterion there is no room for ambiguity. This is the case of the statement "4 is an even number" since there is a well-known and universally accepted definition of even number.

In conclusion, if there is a unique criterion that allows assigning unambiguously truth values to a given declarative sentence, then this sentence is a proposition. In the absence of such unique criterion, the sentence must be accompanied by a qualifying criterion for it to be considered as a proposition.

All the above can be summarized as follows:

> Any proposition is either true or false.
> There is not a third possibility.

Notation

Propositions are usually represented by lowercase letters. The most frequently used letters are *p, q, r, t,* etc. However, sometimes it is convenient to use just one letter with subscripts, such as p_1, p_2, p_3, etc.

The use of notations makes it easier to work with propositions as it avoids repeating the whole statement every time we need to make reference to it. For example, let us have the following proposition: "Parallel lines do not intersect". By making the association between the letter *p* and this statement, it would be enough to say "let's have *p*".

Notations are very useful when we need to refer to indeterminate propositions and not to a particular sentence. Thus, in pointing out "let *p* be any proposition", we are saying that *p* represents any statement. That is, *p* is of variable content the reason why we can say that *p* is a *propositional variable*. Symbols or letters that are used to represent specific statements whose truth values are not determined are also considered as propositional variables. For example,

p: "*x* is an even number."

Only when we say which number *x* is, *p* can be assigned a truth value, and then *p* will become a proposition. Otherwise, while *x* is kept as a variable *p* is also a propositional variable.

As for the truth values a capital **T** is used to indicate "true" and a capital **F** is used to indicate "false". It is also common to encode the use of numbers 1 and 0 to indicate "true" and "false" respectively.

LOGICAL CONNECTIVES

Logical connectives are operators that allow obtaining a new proposition from given propositions which are called *component propositions* and whose truth-values are known. The new proposition is called the *resulting proposition* with truth value being determined by the truth values of the component propositions and the definition of the logical connective applied by the operation.

The above definition is illustrated in Figure 1.1.

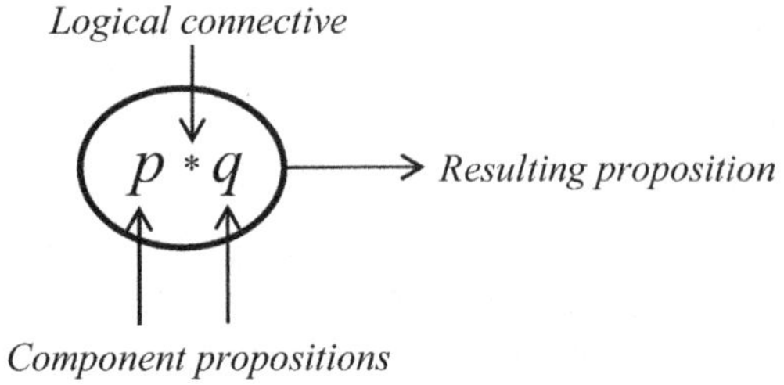

Figure 1.1

From the point of view of logic, we must study how propositions are connected to give rise to a resulting proposition and mainly the relations between the different combinations of truth values of the components and that of the resulting one. This corresponds to the definition of each logical connective. That is, such a definition consists of describing the resulting proposition in terms of the component propositions by indicating the truth value of the new proposition in terms of the truth values of the components.

The logical connectives that are applied to two propositions are called binaries while those applied to a single proposition are known as unitary. We will study six different types of connectives:

$$\text{Unitary} \begin{cases} \text{Negation} \end{cases}$$

$$\text{Binaries} \begin{cases} \text{Conjunction} \\ \text{Inclusive disjunction} \\ \text{Exclusive disjunction} \\ \text{Conditional} \\ \text{Biconditional} \end{cases}$$

Negation is a logical connective that applied to a proposition gives rise to a new proposition whose value of truth is opposite to that of the original proposition. That is, if the given proposition is true, then the resulting proposition is false and vice versa.

To denote the negation of a given proposition p we can use any of the following notations:

$$\sim p, \bar{p}, \neg p, p'$$

In all those cases we read them as "no p".

The relations between the truth values of the component propositions and those of the resulting proposition can be schematized in a table that is known as the *truth table*. For the case of negation, that table is as follows:

p	$\sim p$
T	F
F	T

Negation is the only unary logical connective that we will study.

In ordinary language, the negation of a given proposition can be obtained in various ways depending on the statement of the original proposition. In some cases, the negation can be obtained by placing the word "not" in the grammatically appropriate place. In other cases, it may be more convenient to add the expression "it is not true that" at the beginning of the statement of the original proposition. Sometimes it is also possible to change some words or expressions in the original statement by others with the opposite meanings.

Examples

Given the following proposition:

p: "8 is an odd number."

Any of the following expressions can be a negation of *p*:

~*p*: "8 is **not** an odd number" or

~*p*: "**It is not true** that 8 is an odd number" or

~*p*: "8 is an **even** number."

Let *q* be the following proposition:

q: "Second degree equations always have two solutions."

The following are negations of *q*:

~*q*: "Second degree equations do **not** always have two solutions."

~*q*: "**It is not true that** second degree equations always have two solutions."

Conjunction

The conjunction is a logical connective that applied to two propositions gives rise to a new proposition which is true when the components are both true and it is false in the rest of the cases. It is assigned the symbol "$\wedge$". This way, the conjunction of *p* and *q* can be written as

$$p \wedge q$$

and it is read as "*p* and *q*".

The conjunction is a binary connective like the rest of the connectives that we are going to study in the next sections.

In order to construct the corresponding truth table, it must be taken into account that each proposition has two possible truth values (T or F) so that there are four possible combinations and thus the following table is formed:

p	q	$p \wedge q$
T	T	T
T	F	F
F	T	F
F	F	F

The table above shows the possible combinations of truth values of the given propositions *p* and *q*. As indicated in the above definition, the proposition resulting from a conjunction of two given propositions is true only when both propositions are true, which is reflected in the first row of the table. In all other cases, the resulting proposition is false. In ordinary language the conjunction of two propositions is obtained by joining them with the word "and".

Example 1

Given the following propositions:

p: "6 is an even number."

q: "5 is a prime number."

The conjunction of the two propositions is:

$p \wedge q$: "6 is an even number and 5 is a prime number."

Given the fact that both p and q are true and according to the definition, we can conclude that the resulting proposition is also true.

Example 2

Let us have the propositions:

p: "3 is an even number."

q: "6 is an even number."

The conjunction of both propositions is:

$p \wedge q$: "3 is an even number and 6 is an even number."

We can also write this conjunction as

$p \wedge q$: "3 and 6 are both even numbers."

In this case, we have that p is false while q is true and according to the previous definition, the conjunction $p \wedge q$ is false.

Inclusive disjunction

The inclusive disjunction is a logical connective that applied to two propositions gives rise to a new proposition which is false only when both components are false, and it is true in the remaining cases. It is assigned the symbol "∨". This way, the inclusive disjunction of p and q can be written as

$$p \vee q$$

and it is read "p or q"

In ordinary language, the inclusive disjunction of two propositions is obtained by joining them with the word "or".

The relationship between the truth values of the resulting proposition $p \vee q$ and that of the components is shown in the following truth table:

p	q	$p \vee q$
T	T	T
T	F	T
F	T	T
F	F	F

Example

Let us have the propositions:

p: "15 is a multiple of 3."

q: "15 is a multiple of 2."

The inclusive disjunction of those propositions is:

$p \vee q$: "15 is a multiple of 3 or 15 is a multiple of 2."

The resulting proposition is true since according to the definition it is enough that one of the propositions is true.

Inclusive disjunction indicates alternation and simultaneity because according to its definition it is true if both components are true (simultaneity) or if only one of them is true (alternation).

There are other ways to write the inclusive disjunction of the given propositions. For example, it would be easier to write:

$p \vee q$: "15 is a multiple of 3 or a multiple of 2."

Another way is:

$p \vee q$: "15 is a multiple of 3 or 2."

Exclusive disjunction

The exclusive disjunction is a logical connective that applied to two propositions gives rise to a new proposition which is true only when one of the components is true and the other is false. Therefore, the resulting proposition is false when both propositions have the same truth value. In other words, the exclusive disjunction is true if one component, and only one, is true but not both. It is assigned the symbol "V". This way, the exclusive disjunction of p and q can be written as

$$p \veebar q$$

In ordinary language the exclusive disjunction of two propositions is obtained by writing the word "either" before the first preposition and the word "or" before the second one. Then, it will be read as "either *p* or *q*".

The exclusive disjunction indicates alternation but not simultaneity since it has been said that the resulting proposition is true only when one component is true, and the other is false. That is, the resulting proposition is true only when the truth values of the components are different.

The following table summarizes the definition of the exclusive disjunctive connective:

p	q	$p \veebar q$
T	T	F
T	F	T
F	T	T
F	F	F

Example

Given the following propositions:

p: "4 is an even number."

q: "3 is an odd number."

The exclusive disjunction is:

$p \veebar q$: "either 4 is an even number or 3 is an odd number."

According to the definition, in this example $p \veebar q$ is false because both components are true.

Conditional

To facilitate the understanding of the definition of this important logical connective, let us start with the symbol assigned to it and how to use it. The conditional is represented by the symbol "→". Thus, given the propositions p and q we can write:

$$p \rightarrow q$$

The first proposition (p) is called "antecedent" and the second (q) is known as "consequent".

The conditional is a logical connective that applied to two propositions gives rise to a new proposition which is always true except when the antecedent is true, and the consequent is false. The corresponding truth table is as follows:

p	q	$p \to q$
T	T	T
T	F	F
F	T	T
F	F	T

In ordinary language the conditional of two propositions is obtained by writing the word "if" before the first preposition and the word "then" before the second one. Thus, it will be read as "if p, then q".

It is necessary to emphasize that the order in which the component propositions are written is very important in the case of this connective. That is, exchanging the antecedent and the consequent will produce different resulting propositions. In other words, the conditional is not commutative.

To help understand the definition of the conditional, we rely on the following example:

Example

Given the following propositions:

p: "I study."

q: "I pass the exam."

Let us form the following conditional:

$p \to q$: "If I study, then I pass the exam."

Let us examine each possibility that we can have. We start by assuming that both p and q are true. In this case, the commitment to pass having studied for the exam has been fulfilled. Therefore, the resulting proposition is considered true. In the case of p is true and q false, the process is broken. This means that the commitment to pass having studied for the exam has not been fulfilled. For this reason, in this case, the resulting proposition is considered false. Another possibility is that p is false while q is true. In this situation, it can be said that the commitment to pass the exam has been fulfilled even though the student did not study. That is, the objective was fulfilled even though the antecedent failed to be true. In this way, the resulting proposition is considered true. The last possibility to be considered is when both p and q are false. In other words, this situation corresponds to that in which the student did not study and therefore he or she did not pass the exam. This would be an expected situation and the resulting proposition is also considered as true.

Notice that in the last two cases the antecedent, which is the condition, is not fulfilled. For this reason, fulfilling a commitment is not mandatory. It can be fulfilled or not. The whole explanation given through this example was only for illustrative purposes.

We tried to convey an intuitive idea of a logical connective that is not as obvious as the previous ones. In fact, this explanation could have been omitted, but it was considered useful to get a better understanding.

Biconditional

The biconditional is a logical connective that applied to two propositions gives rise to a new proposition which is true only when both components have the same truth value. Otherwise, it is false. The biconditional connective is represented by the symbol "↔". Thus, given the propositions p and q we can write:

$$p \leftrightarrow q$$

and it is read "p if and only if q".

In ordinary language the biconditional of two propositions is obtained by writing "if and only if" between the first and the second proposition.

The truth table for the biconditional connective is the following:

p	q	$p \leftrightarrow q$
T	T	T
T	F	F
F	T	F
F	F	T

Examples

Let us have the following propositions:

p: "Water does not freeze at any temperature."

q: "17 plus 7 is greater than 20."

The biconditional of *p* and *q* is the following proposition:

$p \leftrightarrow q$: "water does not freeze at any temperature, *if and only if*, 17 plus 7 is greater than 20".

According to the definition, the resulting proposition $p \leftrightarrow q$ is false because *p* is false, and *q* is true (see the corresponding truth table).

Given the propositions:

p: "The real number zero has a multiplicative inverse."

q: "The square root of a negative real number is also a real number."

The corresponding biconditional is:

$p \leftrightarrow q$: "The real number zero has multiplicative inverse, *if and only if*, the square root of a negative real number is also a real number."

The resulting proposition is true since both components have the same truth value (both are false).

It is interesting to note that the logical connectives studied above are enough to cover all possible cases of combinations of two given propositions. This fact can be verified by the table shown below. The table shows all possible combinations of truth values that a resulting proposition can have from the combination of two given propositions by a single connective.

p	q	1	2	3	4	5	6	7	8	9	10	11	12	13	14	15	16
T	**T**	T	T	T	T	T	T	T	T	F	F	F	F	F	F	F	F
T	**F**	T	T	T	T	F	F	F	F	T	T	T	T	F	F	F	F
F	**T**	T	T	F	F	T	T	F	F	T	T	F	F	T	T	F	F
F	**F**	T	F	T	F	T	F	T	F	T	F	T	F	T	F	T	F

Columns 9 through 16 correspond to the negations of columns 1 through 8. Thus, 16 is the negation of 1, 15 is the negation of 2 and so on with 9 being the negation of 8. Columns 1 through 8 correspond as follows:

1. Proposition always true (Tautology)
2. $p \vee q$
3. $q \rightarrow p$
4. p
5. $p \rightarrow q$
6. q
7. $p \leftrightarrow q$
8. $p \wedge q$

Notice the absence of the combination that corresponds to the exclusive disjunction. However, this can be considered the negation of the biconditional (column 7) whose combination is included in column 10. In addition, it can also be noticed that there are two possibilities that correspond to the conditional (columns 3 and 5). This is because this is the only non-commutative logical connective that we have studied here. Thus, when the antecedent and the consequent are exchanged in their positions the corresponding truth table also changes.

PROPOSITIONAL FORMULAS

Propositional formulas are expressions generated by combining a finite number of propositional variables, logical connectives, and grouping symbols. Some examples are:

$$p \wedge q$$

$$p \rightarrow q$$

$$p$$

$$(\sim p \vee \sim q) \rightarrow (p \vee q)$$

$$\sim (p \leftrightarrow q)$$

$$[p \vee (q \wedge r)] \rightarrow q$$

In the previous formulas, we have included propositional variables, logical connectives, and grouping symbols by using the appropriate conventional notation in such a way that they express a complete meaningful content. These are the formulas that are considered well-constructed, which are simply called formulas. This clarification is made because there are poorly constructed expressions which are incomplete and do not express any content or are nonsense expressions such as

$$(\sim p \vee q) \rightarrow$$

It is also important to emphasize the role played by the grouping symbols in the construction of formulas. They show the correct process for constructing formulas that avoid all possible ambiguities. For example, let us have the following expression:

$$p \vee q \wedge r$$

This is an ambiguous and poorly constructed expression because it can be interpreted in two different ways as shown below.

$$(p \vee q) \wedge r \qquad \text{or} \qquad p \vee (q \wedge r)$$

These two formulas lead to two different resulting propositions because they produce different truth tables.

Additionally, grouping symbols allow us to determine or give evidence about what we could consider as the hierarchical position of each connective involved in the formula. That is, it allows visualizing which connective occupies the main position and which ones occupy secondary positions in the same formula. Thus, for example, in the following formula:

$$[(p \vee q) \wedge \mathrm{r}] \rightarrow (\sim \mathrm{p})$$

We can easily see that the main connective is the conditional "→" which is not enclosed by any grouping symbol while the remaining ones are. The correct placement of the grouping symbols makes it clear that the previous formula is a conditional in which both the antecedent and the consequent are formed by a suitable grouping of propositional variables. Then, we can see that the main connective within the formula is the one enclosed by the least number of grouping symbols or by none. In other words, the hierarchical position of each connective within a formula is in inverse relation to the number of grouping symbols that enclose it.

According to their structure, the propositional formulas are classified as atomic or molecular.

Atomic Formulas

This is the type of formula in which only one propositional variable is involved as the unique element of the formula. There is not logical connective or grouping symbol involved. For example, p is an atomic formula.

Molecular Formulas

In these formulas, at least one logical connective intervenes. Examples of molecular formulas are:

$$\sim p$$

$$p \wedge q$$

$$(p \vee q) \wedge r$$

Propositional formulas are denoted by capital letters, such as P, Q, R, etc. According to the definition, we can state that

1) Any propositional variable is a formula.

2) If P and Q are formulas, then

$$\sim P,\ P \wedge Q,\ \mathrm{P} \vee Q,\ P \underline{\vee} Q,\ P \rightarrow Q \text{ and } P \leftrightarrow Q$$

are also formulas.

3) Only the expressions obtained by 1) and 2) are formulas.

Logical reasoning is one of the main objectives of analysis in propositional logic. The structure of logical reasoning is built on propositional formulas. Therefore, the interest is focused on the analysis of the truth values of a given molecular formula in terms of the truth values of the component propositions. For this reason, it is necessary to make a more extensive exposition of the schema called the *truth table* which constitutes the main support tool in this analysis.

Truth tables

To build a truth table we must recall the principle that every propositional variable has only two possible truth values: true or false. Also, we must keep in mind that the truth value of a molecular formula depends on the truth values of its propositional variables.

The table has two parts: one part on the left side that we call the *margin* and the other one on the right side that we call the *body*. We must place the truth values of the propositional variables involved in the formula in the margin. In the body, we gradually write the partial structures of the formula until reaching the complete final structure of the formula. This will be clarified later with examples.

The number of propositional variables involved in a molecular formula determines the number of possible combinations of truth values that will appear in the margin of the table. This total number of combinations is equal to 2^n where the base of this power indicates the number of possible truth values for each propositional variable. The exponent indicates the number of propositional variables involved in the formula. For example, if a certain molecular formula involves three propositional variables, say p, q, and r, the total combinations will be 2^3. Therefore, we will have eight possibilities that will be distributed in the margin of the table as shown below:

p	q	r
T	T	T
T	T	F
T	F	T
T	F	F
F	T	T
F	T	F
F	F	T
F	F	F

In that way, we get the different combinations of truth values of the propositional variables that intervene in any formula. This is how the margin of the table can be mechanically built. What follows is the determination of the truth values of the partial structures of the formula. They are progressively obtained until getting the truth values of the final structure that correspond to each combination of truth values of the propositional variables that are written in each row of the margin. The building process of the table goes following the definitions of the logical connectives that intervene in the formula. The whole process is captured in the body of the table.

The best way to understand the construction process of a truth table is through examples that are given below.

Examples

Let us get the truth tables corresponding to the following formulas:

1. $\sim [p \rightarrow (q \wedge r)]$
2. $r \wedge \sim (p \rightarrow q)$

The corresponding truth tables are as follows:

1.

p	q	r	$q \wedge r$	$p \rightarrow (q \wedge r)$	$\sim [p \rightarrow (q \wedge r)]$
T	**T**	**T**	T	T	F
T	**T**	**F**	F	F	T
T	**F**	**T**	F	F	T
T	**F**	**F**	F	F	T
F	**T**	**T**	T	T	F
F	**T**	**F**	F	T	F
F	**F**	**T**	F	T	F
F	**F**	**F**	F	T	F

The first three columns constitute the margin that is built according to the guides described above. The given formula is a negation of a conditional which goes in the last column. The conditional has p as antecedent and the conjunction $q \wedge r$ as consequent. Therefore, we must write the truth values for this conjunction which must go in the fourth column. The next step is to determine the truth values for the conditional $p \rightarrow (q \wedge r)$ which must go in the fifth column. Finally, the negation of this conditional constitutes the sixth column.

2.

p	q	r	$p \rightarrow q$	$\sim (p \rightarrow q)$	$r \wedge \sim (p \rightarrow q)$
T	**T**	**T**	T	F	F
T	**T**	**F**	T	F	F
T	**F**	**T**	F	T	T
T	**F**	**F**	F	T	F
F	**T**	**T**	T	F	F
F	**T**	**F**	T	F	F
F	**F**	**T**	T	F	F
F	**F**	**F**	T	F	F

In this case, the main connective is a conjunction of the propositions r and the negations of the conditional $p \rightarrow q$. After filling in the first three columns that constitute the margin, the first step is to write the truth values of this conditional in the fourth column. Immediately after this step, we write the truth values corresponding to the negation of this conditional in the fifth column. Finally, the last column is filled with the truth values of the resulting formula which is the given conjunction.

The propositional formulas can also be classified according to the truth values they assume. According to this criterion, we have formulas that are tautologies, contradictions or indeterminate. Let us have a look at each case.

Tautology

A propositional formula constitutes a *tautology*, if and only if, it is always true no matter what the truth values of its components are.

Example

Let us have the following formula:

$$(p \to q) \to (\sim q \to \sim p)$$

The corresponding truth table is the following:

p	q	$\sim p$	$\sim q$	$p \to q$	$\sim q \to \sim p$	$(p \to q) \to (\sim q \to \sim p)$
T	**T**	F	F	T	T	T
T	**F**	F	T	F	F	T
F	**T**	T	F	T	T	T
F	**F**	T	T	T	T	T

We can see that in the last column of the truth table there are only true values. Therefore, this formula is always true regardless of the combination of the truth values of the component propositions. In conclusion, according to the definition given above this formula is a tautology.

A tautology is a formally true proposition. That is, a tautology is always true because of its logical form. In other words, it is always true because of the way in which the component propositions are combined regardless of their truth values. Tautologies are also known as *logical principles* or *universally true propositions.* The role of tautological propositions is crucial in the analysis of logical reasoning precisely because they are not false under any circumstance.

Contradiction

> A propositional formula constitutes a *contradiction*, if and only if, it is always false no matter what the truth values of its components are.

Example

Given the following formula:

$$\sim [p \rightarrow (q \rightarrow p)]$$

The corresponding truth table is the following:

p	q	$q \rightarrow p$	$p \rightarrow (q \rightarrow p)$	$\sim [p \rightarrow (q \rightarrow p)]$
T	**T**	T	T	F
T	**F**	T	T	F
F	**T**	F	T	F
F	**F**	T	T	F

In fact, we can observe that the table shows only false values in its last column. Therefore, the corresponding formula is always false regardless of the combination of the truth values of its component propositions. In conclusion, according to the definition given above this formula is a contradiction.

A contradiction is always false because of its logical form. This is because of the way the component propositions are combined regardless of their truth values. Contradictions are universally false propositions.

It is obvious that the negation of a tautology leads to a contradiction and vice versa. This has also been shown by this example. The formula

$$p \rightarrow (q \rightarrow p)$$

is in fact a tautology (see the fourth column in the truth table) and its negation

$$\sim [p \rightarrow (q \rightarrow p)]$$

is a contradiction (fifth column).

Like tautologies, contradictions play an important role in the analysis of logical reasoning and in mathematical proofs as we will see later in this book.

Indeterminate

A propositional formula is *indeterminate*, if and only if, it is false for some combinations of truth values of its component propositions and true for other combinations, no matter in what proportions these truth values are present.

Example

Given the following formula:

$$(p \rightarrow q) \wedge (q \vee p)$$

The corresponding truth table is the following:

p	q	$p \rightarrow q$	$q \vee p$	$(p \rightarrow q) \wedge (q \vee p)$
T	**T**	T	T	T
T	**F**	F	T	F
F	**T**	T	T	T
F	**F**	T	F	F

This formula is indeterminate since the last column of its truth table shows both true and false values.

Logically Equivalent Formulas

> Two propositional formulas are *logically equivalent*, if and only if, they involve the same propositional variables and the columns corresponding to these formulas in their respective truth tables are identical.

Given the propositional formulas denoted by P and Q. If they are logically equivalent, we write:

$$P \equiv Q$$

this is read as

"Formula P is logically equivalent to formula Q."

When the formulas are not logically equivalent, we write:

$$P \not\equiv Q$$

and it is read as

"Formula P is not logically equivalent to formula Q."

Example

Given the following formulas:

$$\sim p \rightarrow \sim q \qquad p \vee \sim q \qquad \sim p \wedge q$$

Their truth tables are shown below. They are summarized in one since the same propositional variables intervene in all of them.

p	q	$\sim p$	$\sim q$	$\sim p \rightarrow \sim q$	$p \vee \sim q$	$\sim p \wedge q$
T	**T**	F	F	T	T	F
T	**F**	F	T	T	T	F
F	**T**	T	F	F	F	T
F	**F**	T	T	T	T	F

The formulas in columns (5) and (6) are logically equivalent because they have identical truth value distributions for the same combinations of truth values of the component propositions. Then, we can write:

$$(\sim p \rightarrow \sim q) \equiv (p \vee \sim q)$$

$$(\sim p \rightarrow \sim q) \not\equiv (\sim p \wedge q)$$

$$(p \vee \sim q) \not\equiv (\sim p \wedge q)$$

Examples

It can be verified:

$$(p \wedge q) \equiv \sim (\sim p \vee \sim q)$$

This means that we can write conjunction of two given propositions in terms of the negation of the inclusive disjunction of their respective negations.

We can also verify:

$$(p \rightarrow q) \equiv \sim (p \wedge \sim q)$$

Therefore, the conditional can be written in terms of the negation of the conjunction of the antecedent and the negation of the consequent.

An important equivalence is the following:

$$(p \leftrightarrow q) \equiv [(p \rightarrow q) \wedge (q \rightarrow \mathrm{p})]$$

This equivalence allows writing the biconditional in terms of the conjunction and the conditional. This equivalence is very helpful in doing demonstrations.

Another important equivalence is the following:

$$(p \veebar q) \equiv \sim (p \leftrightarrow q)$$

This means that the exclusive disjunction can be written in terms of the negation of the biconditional.

EXERCISES I

1. Determine whether the following statements are propositions. Write those which are proposition symbolically (using symbols), identify the atomic propositions, and the logical connectives that intervene.

   a) This year our College will be better than in previous years.

   b) If the *GDP* (Gross Domestic Product) keeps on decreasing, then the economic growth will be negative this year in our country.

   c) We do not know if it will happen.

   d) Peter, Frank, and Tony were admitted in college this year.

   e) If your expenses are less than your income, then your net savings are positive, and your assets increase.

   f) The high cost of living and the housing problem.

   g) Real wages decrease with inflation.

h) How old are you?

i) If n is an even number and the product n x m is odd, then m is an odd number.

j) If the income from exports starts to decrease, then we must either reduce expenses or increase domestic production.

2. Given the propositions:

   p: "Inflation hurts people with fixed income."

   q: "Inflation destroys the purchasing power."

   r: "The less the government's expenses, the lower the risk of inflation"

   Write in words the following:

   a) $p \rightarrow q$

   b) $(p \wedge q) \rightarrow r$

   c) $(r \vee q) \wedge p$

   d) $\sim q \rightarrow (r \wedge \sim p)$

   e) $\sim r \veebar (p \wedge q)$

   f) $\sim (p \wedge q)$

   g) $p \leftrightarrow (q \wedge r)$

   h) $\sim [p \rightarrow (q \veebar r)]$

3. Given the propositions *p, q* and *r* below, write the statements provided in each of the following cases by using the appropriate symbols:

a)

p: "The supply increases."

q: "The demand decreases."

r: "Prices are stable."

"It is not true that if supply increases and the demand does not decrease, then prices do not remain stable."

b)

p: "Prices are high."

q: "Prices increase."

r: "The cost of living becomes more expensive."

"If the cost of living becomes more expensive, then it is not true that either prices do not rise or that prices are high."

4. By observing the following truth tables, determine how *p* and *q* are connected.

a)

p	*q*	( )
T	**T**	F
T	**F**	F
F	**T**	F
F	**F**	T

b)

p	*q*	( )
T	**T**	F
T	**F**	T
F	**T**	T
F	**F**	T

c)

p	*q*	( )
T	**T**	F
T	**F**	T
F	**T**	F
F	**F**	F

5. Determine which of the statements given below are propositions. Write those that are propositions by using symbols and determine their truth value.

   a) If 4 and 5 are even numbers, then 20 is an odd number.

   b) Inflation hurts people with fixed income and if it destroys their purchasing power, then it deteriorates real wages.

   c) If 3 and 7 are odd numbers, then either 3 is less than 7 or 7 is less than 3.

   d) Either the sum of 7 and 2 is an odd number or 7 and 2 are even numbers.

   e) If even numbers are divisible by 2 and odd numbers are divisible by 3, then the sum of an even number and an odd number is divisible by 6.

6. Knowing that

   i) Galileo was born before Descartes.

   ii) Descartes was born in the XVI century.

   iii) Newton was not born before Shakespeare.

   iv) Racine was not a compatriot of Galileo.

   Determine the truth value of the following statements:

a) If Galileo was born before Descartes, then Newton was born before Shakespeare.

b) If Racine was a compatriot of Galileo or Newton was born before Shakespeare, then Descartes was born in the XVI century.

c) If Racine was not a compatriot of Galileo, then Descartes was not born in the XVI century or Newton was not born before Shakespeare.

7. Say which of the following statements are propositions:

a) If x is greater than 2, then x^2 is greater than 4.

b) Two congruent triangles are similar.

c) Two similar triangles are congruent.

d) Find the area of a triangle whose vertices are (0, 0), (1, 0) and (0, 1).

e) $a\,(b + c) + 3$

f) You can never divide by zero.

8. Translate the following statements into symbolic language:

a) Either the fire was intentionally produced, or it was produced by internal combustion.

b) If John testifies and tells the truth, he will be found guilty and if he does not testify, he will be found guilty.

c) If there are more cats than dogs, then there are more horses than dogs and there are fewer snakes than cats.

9. Answer the following questions:

   a) If for any proposition q, $p \vee q$ is true. What can you say about the truth value of p?

   b) If for any proposition q, $p \wedge q$ is false. What can you say about the truth value of p?

   c) If $p \leftrightarrow q$ is true. What can you say about the truth value of $p \vee \sim q$?

   d) If $p \rightarrow q$ is true. What can you say about the truth value of $p \veebar q$?

   e) If $p \rightarrow q$ is false. What can you say about the truth value of $p \veebar q$?

10. For each of the following situations prove what is asked.

    a) Assuming that the proposition q is false, prove that:

    i) $p \wedge q$ is a contradiction.

    ii) $p \rightarrow q$ is logically equivalent *to* $\sim p$.

    iii) $p \vee q$ is logically equivalent *to* p.

    iv) $\sim p \rightarrow q$ is logically equivalent *to* p.

    b) Assuming that the proposition p is true, prove that:

    i) $p \vee q$ is a tautology.
    ii) $\sim p \wedge q$ is a contradiction.
    iii) $\sim p \vee q$ is logically equivalent *to* q.

11. Given the propositions p, q, r, s, and t such as that both q and r are true while p, s, and t are false, determine the truth value of the following:

    a) $p \rightarrow (q \rightarrow p)$

    b) $[r \rightarrow (\sim q)] \rightarrow (t \vee q)$

    c) $(p \vee q) \rightarrow (\sim p \rightarrow r)$

    d) $p \rightarrow (s \rightarrow t)$

    e) $q \rightarrow (q \veebar s)$

    f) $(p \vee s) \rightarrow s$

12. Determine which of the following propositions are tautologies:

    a) $p \rightarrow (p \vee \sim p)$

    b) $p \rightarrow [q \rightarrow (q \rightarrow p)]$

    c) $(p \rightarrow q) \leftrightarrow (\sim q \rightarrow p)$

    d) $p \leftrightarrow (p \wedge \sim p)$

    e) $[(p \wedge q) \rightarrow (p \wedge \sim p)] \rightarrow (q \vee \sim q)$

    f) $(p \rightarrow q) \leftrightarrow (\sim q \rightarrow \sim p)$

    g) $(p \rightarrow q) \rightarrow (q \rightarrow p)$

    h) $[(p \rightarrow q) \rightarrow p] \rightarrow p$

    i) $(p \rightarrow q) \rightarrow r$

    j) $[(p \wedge q) \rightarrow r] \leftrightarrow [(p \rightarrow (q \rightarrow r)]$

13. Determine which of the following propositional formulas are tautologies, contradictions or indeterminates:

a) $(p \vee r) \wedge (p \rightarrow q)$

b) $(p \rightarrow q) \wedge (r \leftrightarrow p)$

c) $(p \vee q) \leftrightarrow (q \vee r)$

d) $(p \leftrightarrow q) \rightarrow (r \rightarrow q)$

e) $(\sim p \veebar \sim q) \rightarrow [p \wedge (\sim q \leftrightarrow \sim p)]$

f) $[q \rightarrow (\sim p \wedge \sim q)] \rightarrow [\sim p \veebar (q \leftrightarrow \sim p)]$

g) $p \rightarrow \{[(p \vee q) \wedge r] \leftrightarrow [(\sim p \veebar \sim q) \wedge \sim r]\}$

h) $p \wedge [(q \vee r) \rightarrow (\sim p \veebar \sim r)]$

i) $[(p \wedge q) \vee r] \leftrightarrow [p \veebar (\sim r \rightarrow \sim q)]$

j) $[\sim (q \vee r)] \rightarrow [(p \wedge q) \veebar (p \leftrightarrow r)]$

k) $[(p \vee q) \wedge (q \veebar r)] \leftrightarrow [\sim (q \rightarrow p)]$

l) $r \wedge \sim (p \rightarrow q)$

m) $\sim [p \rightarrow (q \wedge r)]$

14. Determine whether the following equivalences are true:

a) $[p \rightarrow (q \vee r)] \equiv [(p \vee q) \rightarrow (p \vee r)]$

b) $[p \rightarrow (q \vee r)] \equiv [(p \rightarrow r) \vee (p \rightarrow q)]$

c) $[(p \wedge q) \rightarrow r] \equiv [(p \rightarrow r) \wedge (q \rightarrow r)]$

d) $[(p \rightarrow q) \wedge (q \rightarrow p)] \equiv (q \leftrightarrow p)$

e) $[\sim (\sim p \vee \sim q)] \equiv (p \wedge q)$

f) $[p \wedge (q \vee r)] \equiv [(r \wedge p) \vee (p \wedge q)]$

g) $(p \veebar q) \equiv [\sim (q \leftrightarrow p)]$

h) $[(q \vee p) \wedge r] \equiv [r \wedge (p \leftrightarrow q)]$

15. Prove the following properties by using truth tables:

a) Associative: $[(p \wedge q) \wedge r] \equiv [p \wedge (q \wedge r)]$
$[(p \vee q) \vee r] \equiv [p \vee (q \vee r)]$

b) Distributive: $[(p \wedge q) \vee r] \equiv [(p \vee r) \wedge (q \vee r)]$
$[(p \vee q) \wedge r] \equiv [(p \wedge r) \vee (q \wedge r)]$

c) Absorption: $[p \wedge (q \vee p)] \equiv p$
$[p \vee (q \wedge p)] \equiv p$

THE CONDITIONAL

Given the fact that the conditional plays an important role in the development of mathematical concepts, definitions and proofs, this section is devoted to studying this logical connective in detail.

First, we are going to focus our attention on what we call the *derived forms of a conditional.* These are the different conditionals that can be obtained from a given conditional. The most important derived forms are:

The statement (also called the direct form)
This is the conditional given originally: $P \rightarrow Q$.

The converse
It is obtained by exchanging the antecedent and the consequent in the given conditional: $Q \to P$.

The inverse (also called the contrary of the direct)
This form is obtained by the negation of both the antecedent and the consequent of the original conditional: $\sim P \to \sim Q$.

The contrapositive
It is obtained by the negation of both the antecedent and the consequent of the converse form: $\sim Q \to \sim P$.

The corresponding truth tables are summarized as follows:

P	Q	$\sim P$	$\sim Q$	$P \to Q$	$Q \to P$	$\sim P \to \sim Q$	$\sim Q \to \sim P$
T	**T**	F	F	T	T	T	T
T	**F**	F	T	F	T	T	F
F	**T**	T	F	T	F	F	T
F	**F**	T	T	T	T	T	T

From the table we can see that

$$(P \to Q) \equiv (\sim Q \to \sim P)$$
$$(Q \to P) \equiv (\sim P \to \sim Q)$$

This also confirms that the conditional is not commutative. The *statement or direct* form and the *converse* are not logically equivalent neither are the *contrapositive* and the *inverse*.

Figure 1.2 shows the relationships between the forms derived from a given conditional.

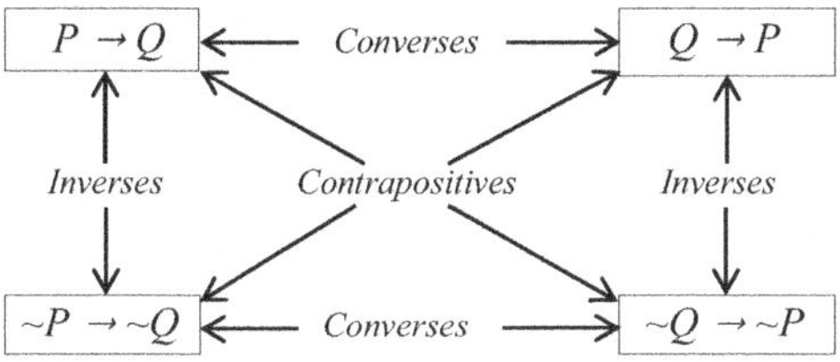

Figure 1.2.

Example

Given the following conditional:

"If an integer ends in zero, then it is an even number."

The derived forms are:

Statement (or given):

"If an integer ends in zero, then it is an even number."

Converse:

"If a number is even, then it ends in zero."

Inverse:

"If an integer doesn't end in zero, then it is not an even number"

Contrapositive:

"If an integer is not even, then it doesn't end in zero."

The above example provides a good way of verifying the equivalences between the derived forms of the conditional. We can observe that the *statement* and the *contrapositive* forms are both true while the *converse* and the *inverse* forms are both false. We can also verify with this example that the conditional is not commutative. In fact, the *statement* form is true, but the *converse* is false whereas the *inverse* is false, and the *contrapositive* is true. Therefore, knowing the truth value of a given conditional and the equivalences between its derived forms makes it easy to determine the truth value of any of them.

EXERCISES II

1. Write the derived forms of the following conditionals:

   a) If a and b are both odd numbers, then $a - b$ is an even number.

   b) If inflation destroys the purchasing power, then the living cost increases with inflation.

   c) If n is divisible by 3, then n is divisible by 9.

   d) If a country's exports are greater than its imports, then its balance of payments is negative.

   e) If the labor market is perfectly competitive, then wages in the same type of job are the same.

   f) If an integer number is divisible by 5, then it ends in 5.

   g) If ABC is an isosceles triangle, then ABC is an equilateral triangle.

   h) If a^2 is an even number, then a is even.

   i) If his net savings are positive and his assets increase, then his expenses are less than his income.

2. Determine the truth values of the derived forms of the following conditionals for each indicated case:

   a) If a is an integer ending in 4, then a is an even number ($a = 12$).

   b) If a is an odd number, then a is multiple of 5 ($a = 13$).

c) If a is an integer multiple of 4, then a is an even number ($a = 2$).

d) If a and b are even numbers, then $a + b$ is an even number ($a = 5$ and $b = 7$).

IMPLICATION

At the beginning of this chapter, we stated that logic studies the forms, structures, or schemes of formal reasoning and that it focuses on what makes it valid or not. In general, we can say that most reasonings are frequently stated in the following way:

"If P, then Q"

Being P and Q propositions.

This means that the reasoning can usually be symbolized by a conditional

"$P \rightarrow Q$"

Therefore, reasoning validity is associated with the truth of the conditional. Therefore, special attention must be given to those conditionals which are always true. As discussed earlier, these types of conditionals are tautologies, and we call them *implications*.

To denote when a conditional is an implication the symbol "$\Rightarrow$" will be used. Thus, given the propositions P and Q we write:

$$P \Rightarrow Q$$

and it is read:

"P implies Q."

The formal definition is as follows:

> Given the propositions P and Q, if the conditional $P \rightarrow Q$ is a tautology we say that P *implies* Q, and we write:
>
> $$P \Rightarrow Q$$

Like the conditional, in the implication P is also called the antecedent and Q the consequent.

According to this definition, an implication occurs if the given conditional is true. This means that the combination of a true antecedent and a false consequent is excluded from all possible combinations of truth values of the conditional components. Thus, by recalling the truth table of the conditional, the following shows the cases in which an implication can occur:

P	Q	$P \Rightarrow Q$
T	**T**	T
F	**T**	T
F	**F**	T

According to what was discussed earlier, there are two ways for an implication to be constituted. One way is when the conditional is always true because of the structure of the formula no matter what the specific statements of the component propositions are. The other way is when it is a tautology because of the specific statements or contents of the component propositions.

Examples

1. Let us have the following formula:

$$[(p \rightarrow q) \wedge p] \rightarrow q$$

The main connective is a conditional. The corresponding truth table is the following:

p	q	$p \rightarrow q$	$(p \rightarrow q) \wedge p$	$[(p \rightarrow q) \wedge p] \rightarrow q$
T	**T**	T	T	T
T	**F**	F	F	T
F	**T**	T	F	T
F	**F**	T	F	T

Since this conditional is a tautology, we can say that it constitutes an implication, and we can write:

$$[(p \rightarrow q) \wedge p] \Rightarrow q$$

We can see that this conditional is always true because of the structure of the formula. It does not matter what the specific statements of p and q are. They can state anything, and the resultant proposition will be always true. The truth of this conditional depends only on the way the formula was constructed.

2. Let us now consider the following statements:

   "If today is Saturday, then tomorrow will be Sunday."

   "If a number is multiple of 25, then it will be multiple of 5."

   "If a number is less than 1, then it is less than 3."

   Those statements constitute conditionals that are always true because there is no way that the consequent to be false if the antecedent is true. Therefore, they are implications. These are examples of conditionals that are always true because of the specific statements of the component propositions.

The conditionals of the last example are implications because of the content of the component propositions. This type of implication plays a very important role in Mathematics as we will see later. In Mathematics, this type of implication is called *theorem*, the antecedent is known as the *hypothesis*, and the consequent is called the *thesis*. Thus, given the theorem:

$$P \Rightarrow Q$$

P is the hypothesis and Q is the thesis.

NECESSITY AND SUFFICIENCY

Let us recall the truth table that shows when the conditional becomes an implication.

P	Q	$P \Rightarrow Q$
T	T	T
F	T	T
F	F	T

We are going to focus the attention on how the truth of one component relates to the truth of the other for the conditional to be true. We can observe that when P is true Q must be true for the conditional to be true. There is not any other option. This happens only in the first row. If Q was false being P true, then the conditional would be false, a situation that is not possible in this case since we are considering an implication. Therefore, we say that it is *sufficient* that P is true for Q to be true.

On the other hand, it is not necessary that P is true for the conditional to be true. If P is false, then Q can be either true or false and the conditional is true in both cases (second and third rows). However, it is *necessary* that Q is true for P to be true. If Q was false, then P must be false as well for the conditional to be true (third row). Even if Q is true, this condition *is not sufficient* for P to be true since P could be false, and the conditional would still be true (second row). This analysis supports the following definition:

> Given the implication $P \Rightarrow Q$.
>
> P is a *sufficient condition* for Q, and
>
> Q is a *necessary condition* for P

Example

Given the following implication:

"If it is raining, then it is cloudy."

We can say that it is *sufficient* that it is raining for it to be cloudy while it is *necessary* that it is cloudy for it to be raining. Of course, it is not sufficient that it is cloudy to be raining.

DOUBLE IMPLICATION

Given the propositions P and Q if it happens:

$$P \Rightarrow Q \qquad \text{and} \qquad Q \Rightarrow P$$

Then we can say that there is a *double implication between P and Q*, and we can write

$$P \Leftrightarrow Q$$

The double implication is read as

"*P* if and only if *Q*"

When there is a double implication between P and Q, we have that $P \Rightarrow Q$ which means that P is a sufficient condition for Q. Also, we have that $Q \Rightarrow P$ which means that in addition P is a necessary condition for Q. Therefore, we can say that P is a necessary and sufficient condition for Q. The same conclusion is true for Q with respect to P. Then, we can state the following definition:

Given the double implication $P \Leftrightarrow Q$.

P is a *necessary and sufficient condition* for Q, and
Q is a *necessary and sufficient condition* for P

Example

Let us have the following implications:

"If a number is even, then it is divisible by 2."

"If a number is divisible by 2, then it is an even number."

Obviously, they constitute a double implication that can be written as

"A number is even, if and only if, it is divisible by 2."

Therefore, we can say that it is necessary and sufficient that a number is divisible by 2 for that number to be even and that it is necessary and sufficient that a number is even for that number to be divisible by 2.

In fact, the previous double implication constitutes the formal definition of an even number.

FORMAL TRUTH AND EMPIRICAL TRUTH

We have stated many times earlier that any propositional formula is either true or false. However, we must distinguish those propositions whose truth-values are the result of their logical form or structure, like tautologies and contradictions, from those whose truth-values depend on the variations of the statements. These are indeterminates.

The truth of the former is what we call a formal truth because it depends only on the way the component propositions are connected regardless of their statements. The truth of the indeterminate is relative and to prove it we must check the statements with facts or experience. Therefore, the truth of indeterminates is called an empirical truth.

Then, to determine if a formula is formally true, we only need to analyze its form or structure. On the contrary, to decide if a formula is empirically true, we need to compare the statements with facts of reality.

Logic is not a science that allows determining if a given formula is empirically true. This is the objective of factual sciences which are interested in studying the facts of reality. Logic is devoted to the study of formal truths, their structures, and laws which allow determining whether a given formula is formally true or not.

What has been said lets us know about the relevance of tautologies in the study of logic. Even more, we can state:

Logic is the study of tautologies.

LOGICAL INFERENCE

Logic provides the principles of reasoning. It establishes a theory of inference. The inference is a logical process of deriving a proposition called a conclusion, from a set of propositions called premises. The premises are accepted as being true, and as a logical consequence, the conclusion will also be true.

The premises can be of the following types:

1) Truths obtained from the experience as it happens in the factual sciences.

2) Accepted truths which are called *axioms*.

3) Previously proven truths known as *theorems*.

To derive a conclusion from given premises, it is necessary to apply a set of rules which are called *rules of inference.* The procedure for getting a true conclusion from premises that are accepted as being true, by applying rules of inference, is known as *deductive reasoning*. Thus, logic provides the criteria which allow us to establish the validity of deductive reasoning. These criteria pay attention only to the form through which they are presented, regardless of the statements of their component propositions. Therefore, our interest is focused on the rules that we can use in deductive reasoning.

Recalling that tautologies are always true because of their structure regardless of the statements, what has been said above evidence the important role that tautologies play in inference. This important role is precisely given by the fact that tautologies do not have empirical content.

LAWS OF LOGIC

> Any formula that is a tautology constitutes a
> *law of the propositional logic*

The laws of logic are the theoretical basis for the rules that govern correct reasoning. These rules are called *rules of inference*.
Therefore, every tautology originates a rule of inference and since there is an infinite number of tautologies, we also have infinite rules of inference available.

It is necessary to verify which rule of inference has been used at each step of the deductive procedure. Therefore, the greater the number of rules the more difficult this verification will be. Fortunately, only a reduced number of inference rules are necessary for deductive reasoning.

The link between the laws of logic (tautologies) and the rules of inference can be explained as follows: A deductive reasoning can be represented by a conditional in which the antecedent is the conjunction of all premises and the consequent is the conclusion. Since it is assumed that all premises are true, to prove that the conclusion is also true it is necessary and sufficient that this conditional is a tautology. In other words, this conditional must be an implication.

In this way, we get the following definition:

Given the deductive reasoning constituted by the premises $P_1, P_2 \ldots P_n$ and the conclusion C, we say that this reasoning is *valid or correct* when:

$$(P_1 \wedge P_2 \wedge \ldots \wedge P_n) \Rightarrow C$$

We can also write the deductive reasoning symbolically as follows:

$$\begin{array}{c} P_1 \\ P_2 \\ \vdots \\ P_n \\ \hline \therefore C \end{array}$$

The symbol $\therefore$ can be read either "Then" or "Therefore".

It was said above that although there are infinite rules of inference, only a few of them are necessary for deductive reasoning. We are going to discuss some of them below.

The most used rules are those called *Syllogisms* in which there are two premises and a conclusion. One of the premises is considered as *the major* and the other is regarded as *the minor*.

The first rules we are going to discuss are called Conditional Syllogisms because one of the two premises is a conditional (the major), while the other is a single proposition (the minor) that affirms or denies either the antecedent or the consequent of the conditional.

Conditional Syllogisms

Modus Ponendo Ponens (MPP)

From Latin this means "The modus that affirms by affirming". The structure is as follows:

$$\begin{array}{l} P \rightarrow Q \\ \underline{P \quad\quad} \\ \therefore\ Q \end{array}$$

Any reasoning structured in that way is valid because in fact:

$$[(P \rightarrow Q) \wedge P] \Rightarrow Q$$

This implication can be proven by building the truth table.

P	Q	$P \rightarrow Q$	$(P \rightarrow Q) \wedge P$	$[(P \rightarrow Q) \wedge P] \Rightarrow Q$
T	**T**	T	T	T
T	**F**	F	F	T
F	**T**	T	F	T
F	**F**	T	F	T

The rule works as follows: If a conditional is accepted as true whose antecedent is also accepted as true, then we can conclude that the consequent must be true (see the corresponding truth table for the conditional).

Example

Let us have the following reasoning:

"If the exam is too long, then students get tired and stop thinking properly. The exam is too long. Then, students get tired and stop thinking properly."

To symbolize this reasoning, we must first identify the component propositions as follows:

p: "The exam is too long."

q: "Students get tired."

r: "Students stop thinking properly."

Thus, the given reasoning can be expressed in symbols as

$$\begin{array}{l} 1)\ p \rightarrow (q \wedge r) \\ 2)\ p \\ \hline \therefore \quad q \wedge r \end{array}$$

We can see that this reasoning has been given according to the MPP rule which allows us to affirm that it is valid. This is, by assuming that premises 1) and 2) are both true we are can conclude that the conjunction of q and r is also true.

Modus Tollendo Tollens (MTT)

The corresponding translation would be "The modus that denies by denying" and its form is as follows:

$$\begin{array}{l} P \rightarrow Q \\ \sim Q \\ \hline \therefore \sim P \end{array}$$

This is a valid way of structuring a reasoning because in fact:

$$[(P \rightarrow Q) \wedge \sim Q] \Rightarrow \sim P$$

This implication can be verified by the following truth table:

P	Q	$\sim P$	$\sim Q$	$P \rightarrow Q$	$(P \rightarrow Q) \wedge \sim Q$	$[(P \rightarrow Q) \wedge \sim Q] \Rightarrow \sim P$
T	**T**	F	F	T	F	T
T	**F**	F	T	F	F	T
F	**T**	T	F	T	F	T
F	**F**	T	T	T	T	T

The rule that we get from this tautology can be expressed in words as follows: If a conditional is accepted as true along with the truth of the negation of its consequent, then we can conclude that the negation of its antecedent must be true.

This is, accepting that $\sim Q$ is true means that we accept that Q is false. Since Q is the consequent of the conditional that we have accepted also as true leads us to accept that the antecedent P must be also false. Therefore, $\sim P$ must be true which is the conclusion.

Example

Let us see the following reasoning:

"If it is raining, I don't go out. I go out. Then, it is not raining."

We identify the propositions with symbols as follows:

p: "It is raining."

q: "I don't go out."

Therefore, in symbols the reasoning looks as follows:

$$\begin{array}{l} 1)\ p \to q \\ 2)\ \sim q \\ \hline \therefore \sim p \end{array}$$

This reasoning has been given according to the MTT rule which allows us to affirm that it is valid. Therefore, if we accept that premises 1) and 2) are both true, then we can conclude that the negation of p is also true.

Disjunctive Syllogisms

This type of syllogism has a disjunction as its major premise. Depending on whether the disjunction is inclusive or exclusive we can have different forms. Let us see them.

Modus Tollendo Ponens (MTP)

This means: "The modus that affirms by denying". This method can be presented in any of following forms:

$$\begin{array}{c} P \vee Q \\ \sim P \\ \hline \therefore Q \end{array} \qquad \begin{array}{c} P \vee Q \\ \sim Q \\ \hline \therefore P \end{array} \qquad \begin{array}{c} P \veebar Q \\ \sim P \\ \hline \therefore Q \end{array} \qquad \begin{array}{c} P \veebar Q \\ \sim Q \\ \hline \therefore P \end{array}$$

The corresponding implications are the followings:

$$[(P \vee Q) \wedge \sim P] \Rightarrow Q \qquad [(P \vee Q) \wedge \sim Q] \Rightarrow P$$

$$[(P \veebar Q) \wedge \sim P] \Rightarrow Q \qquad [(P \veebar Q) \wedge \sim Q] \Rightarrow P$$

We invite the student to prove these implications by building the corresponding truth tables as it was done for the previous cases. Also, as an exercise, the student can do the same for the next cases where these proofs will be omitted.

The following rule is derived from the above implications: If an inclusive (exclusive) disjunction of two propositions is accepted as true along with truth of the negation of one of its components, then we can conclude that the other component must be true.

Focusing the attention on the first form, the reasoning works as follows: if we accept that $\sim P$ is true, then P is false. Therefore, since we have accepted the disjunction $\mathrm{P} \vee Q$ as true, the other component Q must be true, which is the conclusion. The same reasoning applies to the other three forms.

Example

Given the following reasoning:

"Water boils at 50°C or 100°C. Water does not boil at 50°C. Then, water boils at 100°C"

Making the association with symbols we have

p: "Water boils at 50°C"

q: "Water boils at 100°C"

Thus, the symbolic expression of this reasoning is a follow:

$$\begin{array}{l} 1)\ \ p \vee q \\ 2)\ \ \sim p \\ \hline \quad \therefore q \end{array}$$

Therefore, if we accept that 1) and 2) are both true, according to the MTP rule the proposition q: "water boils at 100°C" must be true.

Modus Ponendo Tollens (MPT)

This is the "modus that denies by affirming". The major premise in this method is an exclusive disjunction. The possible forms are the following:

$$\begin{array}{l} P \veebar Q \\ P \\ \hline \therefore \sim Q \end{array} \qquad \text{or} \qquad \begin{array}{l} P \veebar Q \\ Q \\ \hline \therefore \sim P \end{array}$$

The corresponding implications are the following:

$[(P \veebar Q) \wedge P] \Rightarrow \sim Q$ and $[(P \veebar Q) \wedge Q] \Rightarrow \sim P$

The rule is that if an exclusive disjunction of two propositions is accepted as true along with the truth of one of them, then the other proposition must be false, therefore its negation is true which is the conclusion.
Example

Let us have the following reasoning:

"John is either in Paris or in London today. He is in London today. Then, John is not in Paris today."

Identifying the propositions as follows:

p: "John is in Paris today."

q: "John is in London today."

The given reasoning expressed in symbols is like this:

1) $p \veebar q$
2) q

$\therefore \sim p$

Therefore, if we accept that premises 1) and 2) are both true, according to the MPT rule, we can conclude that the negation of p is also true.

Hypothetical Syllogism (HS)

In this type of syllogism premises and conclusion are conditionals. The conditionals assumed as premises are such that the consequent of one is the antecedent of the other. The conclusion is a conditional such that its antecedent is the antecedent of the former and its consequent is the consequent of the latter. In symbols, it is like this:

$$\begin{array}{r} P \rightarrow Q \\ Q \rightarrow R \\ \hline \therefore P \rightarrow R \end{array}$$

The corresponding implication is the following:

$$[(P \rightarrow Q) \wedge (Q \rightarrow R)] \Rightarrow (P \rightarrow R)$$

The derived rule is: If two conditionals are both true, and the consequent of one of them is the antecedent of the other, then we can conclude that the conditional built with the antecedent of the first one as its antecedent and the consequent of the second one as its consequent is also true. This is transitivity.

The reasoning works as follows:

If P is true, Q must be true because we have accepted that $P \rightarrow Q$ is true. Since Q is true, then R must be true because we have accepted that $Q \rightarrow R$ is also true. Therefore, P true and R true means that $P \rightarrow R$ is true.

If P is false, Q must be also false because $P \rightarrow Q$ is accepted as true. So, Being Q false, then R must be also false since $Q \rightarrow R$ is a premise accepted as true. Therefore, P false and R false means that $P \rightarrow R$ is again true. We can see that in all cases the conclusion $P \rightarrow R$ is true.

Example

Let us have the following reasoning:

"If n is an integer that ends in zero, n is divisible by 2. If n is divisible by 2, n is even. Then, if n is an integer that ends in zero, n is even."

By assigning symbols to each proposition, we get

p: "n is an integer that ends in zero."

q: "n is divisible by 2."

r: "n is even."

Thus, the symbolic expression is like this:

$$\begin{array}{l} 1)\ p \rightarrow q \\ 2)\ q \rightarrow r \\ \hline \therefore\ p \rightarrow r \end{array}$$

Therefore, since 1) and 2) are true, we conclude, according to the HS rule, that the conditional $p \rightarrow r$: "If n is an integer that ends in zero, n is even" is also true.

Conjunctive-Disjunctive Syllogism (CDS)

This is a special type of syllogism in which the major premise is a conjunction of two conditionals while the minor premise is an inclusive disjunction. The symbolic form is like this:

$$\begin{array}{l} (P \rightarrow R) \wedge (Q \rightarrow S) \\ P \vee Q \\ \hline \therefore\ R \vee S \end{array}$$

It can also be presented in the following way:

$$\begin{array}{l} (P \rightarrow R) \\ (Q \rightarrow S) \\ P \vee Q \\ \hline \therefore R \vee S \end{array}$$

The corresponding implication is the following:

$$[(P \to R) \wedge (Q \to S) \wedge (P \vee Q)] \Rightarrow (R \vee S)$$

The rule that we obtain from this implication is the following: If two conditionals are both true and the inclusive disjunction of their respective antecedents is also true, the we can conclude that the inclusive disjunction of their respective consequents is true.

The reasoning works as follows: If we accept as premises any two conditionals, which means that we accept that both are true, and also we accept that at least one of the two antecedents must be true or both, then at least one of the two consequent is true or both (recall the truth table of the conditional).

Example

Given the following reasoning:

"If a number *n* is even, then that number is divisible by 2, and if it is an integer that ends in 5, then it is divisible by 5. The integer *n* is even or ends in 5. Then, it is divisible by 2 or 5".

Let us identify the component propositions with symbols as follows:

p: "*n* is even."

q: "*n* is divisible by 2."

r: "*n* is an integer that ends in 5."

s: "*n* is divisible by 5."

Thus, the symbolic expression of this reasoning is as follows:

1) $(p \to q) \wedge (r \to s)$

2) $p \vee r$

$\therefore q \vee s$

Therefore, accepting 1) and 2) as premises, according to the CDS rule, we can conclude that the inclusive disjunction $q \vee s$: "n is divisible by 2 or 5" is also true.

The following rules are very useful in mathematical proofs as we will see later. Therefore, although they seem to be obvious rules, it is worth presenting them here to complete this section.

Double negation (DN)

$$\frac{P}{\therefore \sim(\sim P)}$$

The corresponding implication is the following:

$$P \Rightarrow \sim(\sim P)$$

In words the rule is: If a given proposition is true, we can conclude that its double negation is also true. Another way of stating this rule is: "If a given proposition is true, we can conclude that it is not true that its negation is true."

Simplification (S)

$$\frac{P \wedge Q}{\therefore P} \qquad \text{or} \qquad \frac{P \wedge Q}{\therefore Q}$$

The rule is: If the conjunction of two propositions is true, we can conclude that any of its components is also true. The respective implications are:

$$(P \wedge Q) \Rightarrow P \qquad \text{and} \qquad (P \wedge Q) \Rightarrow Q$$

Conjunction (C)

$$\begin{array}{c} P \\ Q \\ \hline \therefore P \wedge Q \end{array}$$

The implication is the following:

$$(P \wedge Q) \Rightarrow (P \wedge Q)$$

The rule is: If two given propositions are both true, we can conclude that their conjunction is also true.

Addition (A)

$$\frac{P}{\therefore P \vee Q}$$

The implication is this:

$$P \Rightarrow (P \vee Q)$$

The rule: If a given proposition is true, we can conclude that its inclusive disjunction with any other proposition is also true.

LAWS OF EQUIVALENCE

We have said earlier that two propositional formulas are logically equivalent if the columns corresponding to the formula in their respective truth tables are identical to each other. Then, if we recall that the resulting proposition from connecting two propositions by a biconditional is true when the two components have equal truth values, we can conclude that connecting two propositional formulas which are logically equivalent by a biconditional must generate a tautology.

These tautologies are called *Laws of Equivalence.* Like the rules discussed above, these laws are useful in deductive reasoning. Additional rules of inference can also be obtained from them. In this way, we can substitute a formula with another logically equivalent in any deductive reasoning procedure without changing the conclusion.

The following are the most used laws of this type.

Identity (I)

$P \vee F \equiv P$ (F is a Contradiction)

$P \wedge T \equiv P$ (T is a Tautology)

Idempotence (Idem)

$P \vee P \equiv P$

$P \wedge P \equiv P$

Commutative (Comm)

$P \vee Q \equiv Q \vee P$

$P \underline{\vee} Q \equiv Q \underline{\vee} P$

$P \wedge Q \equiv Q \wedge P$

Associative (Assoc)

$(P \wedge Q) \wedge R \equiv P \wedge (Q \wedge R)$

$(P \vee Q) \vee R \equiv P \vee (Q \vee R)$

$(P \underline{\vee} Q) \underline{\vee} R \equiv P \underline{\vee} (Q \underline{\vee} R)$

Distributive (Distr)

$[P \wedge (Q \vee R)] \equiv [(P \wedge Q) \vee (P \wedge R)]$

$[P \vee (Q \wedge R)] \equiv [(P \vee Q) \wedge (P \vee R)]$

De Morgan (De M)

$\sim (P \wedge Q) \equiv \sim P \vee \sim Q$

$\sim (P \vee Q) \equiv \sim P \wedge \sim Q$

Exportation (Exp)

$[(P \wedge Q)] \rightarrow R] \equiv [(P \rightarrow (Q \rightarrow R)]$

After having studied all these laws of logic and their respective rules of inference, we need to see how they can be used to prove the validity of reasoning. The following examples show how to do that.

Examples

1. Let us have the following reasoning:

   "If n is an integer divisible by 8, n is divisible by 4. If n is divisible by 4, n is even. The integer n is not even. Therefore, n is not divisible by 8."

   Let us now associate symbols to the propositions that intervene in the given reasoning as follows:

   p: "n is an integer divisible by 8."

   q: "n is divisible by 4."

   r: "n is even."

   Thus, the symbolic expression of the given reasoning is:

$$\begin{array}{l} a)\ p \rightarrow q \\ b)\ q \rightarrow r \\ \underline{c)\ \sim r} \\ \therefore \sim p \end{array}$$

   To formally prove whether this reasoning is valid or not we have to analyze its structure no matter what the specific statements say. We must indicate the laws or rules which lead us to justify the conclusion.

   In this case, we can see that applying the Hypothetical Syllogism (HS) to premises *a)* and *b)* we can get:

$$b')\ p \rightarrow r$$

Then, applying the Modus Tollendo Tollens (MTT) to premises *b')* and *c)*, leads us to the conclusion $\sim p$.

The above analysis can be presented schematically as follows:

$$
\begin{array}{lll}
a) & p \rightarrow q & \\
b) & q \rightarrow r & \\
b') & p \rightarrow r & \text{(by SH to } a \text{ and } b\text{)} \\
c) & \sim r & \\
\hline
\therefore & \sim p & \text{(by MTT to } b' \text{ and } c\text{)}
\end{array}
$$

This way we have proven that the given reasoning is valid. Notice that we only say whether the reasoning is valid or not, we do not say that it is true or false.

2. Let us now analyze the following reasoning:

   "If North Korea is a democratic country, then the people are free, and the government is elected by the majority. If North Korea is not a democratic country, then the North Korean government has been imposed. The North Korean people are not free, or the North Korean government is not elected by the majority. Therefore, the North Korean government has been imposed".

   Let us identify the propositions that intervene in the given reasoning as follows:

   p: "North Korea is a democratic country."

   q: "The North Korean people are free."

   r: "The North Korean government is elected by the majority."

   s: "The North Korean government has been imposed."

   Thus, the symbolic expression of the given reasoning is:

$$
\begin{array}{l}
a)\ \ p \rightarrow (q \wedge r) \\
b)\ \ \sim p \rightarrow s \\
c)\ \ \sim q \vee \sim r \\
\hline
\therefore\ \ s
\end{array}
$$

The De Morgan (De M) law allows substituting premise *c)* by

$$c')\sim (q \wedge r)$$

According to the Modus Tollendo Tollens (MTT) from premises *a)* and *c')* we get:

$$c'')\sim p$$

Finally, applying the Modus Ponendo Ponens (MPP) to *b)* and *c'')* lead us to conclusion *s*. We can summarize the analysis described above as follows:

$$
\begin{array}{ll}
a)\ \ p \rightarrow (q \wedge r) & \\
b)\ \ \sim p \rightarrow s & \\
c)\ \ \sim q \vee \sim r & \\
c')\sim (q \wedge r) & \text{(De M to } c\text{)} \\
c'')\sim p & \text{(MTT to } a \text{ and } c'\text{)} \\
\hline
\therefore\ \ s & \text{(MPP to } b \text{ and } c''\text{)}
\end{array}
$$

Therefore, the given reasoning is valid.

3. Let us see the following reasoning given in symbolic form:

$$
\begin{array}{l}
a)\ \ p \vee q \\
b)\ \ \sim p \\
c)\ \ r \rightarrow \sim q \\
\hline
\therefore r
\end{array}
$$

By applying the same procedure as we did in previous examples lead us to the following summary of the analysis:

$$p \vee q$$

$$\sim p$$

$$b') \; q \qquad \text{(MTP to } a \text{ and } b\text{)}$$

$$r \rightarrow \sim q$$

$$\therefore \sim r \qquad \text{(MTT to } c \text{ and } b'\text{)}$$

We can see that the application of the rules of inferences is telling us that the correct conclusion is $\sim r$ instead of r. Therefore, the given reasoning is not valid.

The validity of a given deductive reasoning can also be proved by using truth tables. It is enough to prove that the conjunction of all premises implies the conclusion. We do this in the following examples:

4. Let us see again the reasoning given in Example 1.

$$a) \; p \rightarrow q$$

$$b) \; q \rightarrow r$$

$$c) \; \sim r$$

$$\therefore \; \sim p$$

The corresponding conditional is the following:

$$[(p \rightarrow q) \wedge (q \rightarrow r) \wedge \sim r] \rightarrow \sim p$$

And the respective truth table is this:

p	q	r	$\sim p$	$\sim r$	$p \to q$	$q \to r$	$(p \to q) \land (q \to r) \land \sim r$
T	**T**	**T**	F	F	T	T	F
T	**T**	**F**	F	T	T	F	F
T	**F**	**T**	F	F	F	T	F
T	**F**	**F**	F	T	F	T	F
F	**T**	**T**	T	F	T	T	F
F	**T**	**F**	T	T	T	F	F
F	**F**	**T**	T	F	T	T	F
F	**F**	**F**	T	T	T	T	T

$(p \to q) \land (q \to r) \land \sim r$	$\sim p$	$[(p \to q) \land (q \to r) \land \sim r] \to \sim p$
F	F	T
F	F	T
F	F	T
F	F	T
F	T	T
F	T	T
F	T	T
T	T	T

In fact, the corresponding conditional is a tautology which means that it is an implication, and this proves that the given reasoning is valid.

5. Let us now consider the reasoning given in Example 3.

$$\begin{array}{ll} a) & p \vee q \\ b) & \sim p \\ c) & r \rightarrow \sim q \\ \hline & \therefore r \end{array}$$

With the premises and the conclusion, let us form the conditional:

$$[(p \vee q) \wedge (\sim p) \wedge (r \rightarrow \sim q)] \rightarrow r$$

The corresponding truth table is the following:

p	q	r	$\sim p$	$\sim q$	$p \vee q$	$r \rightarrow \sim q$	$[(p \vee q) \wedge (\sim p) \wedge (r \rightarrow \sim q)]$
T	**T**	**T**	F	F	T	F	F
T	**T**	**F**	F	F	T	T	F
T	**F**	**T**	F	T	T	T	F
T	**F**	**F**	F	T	T	T	F
F	**T**	**T**	T	F	T	F	F
F	**T**	**F**	T	F	T	T	T
F	**F**	**T**	T	T	F	T	F
F	**F**	**F**	T	T	F	T	F

$(p \vee q) \wedge (\sim p) \wedge (r \rightarrow \sim q)$	r	$[(p \vee q) \wedge (\sim p) \wedge (r \rightarrow \sim q)] \rightarrow r$
F	T	T
F	F	T
F	T	T
F	F	T
F	T	T
T	F	F
F	T	T
F	F	T

The fact that the corresponding conditional does not constitute an implication proves that the given reasoning is not valid.

EXERCISES III

1. By using symbols write and analyze the validity of the following reasoning:

   a) If n is an integer divisible by 8, n is divisible by 4. If n is divisible by 4, then n is even. The integer n is not even. Therefore, n is not divisible by 8.

   b) If n is an integer divisible by 12, then n is divisible by 6. If n is divisible by 6, then n is divisible by 3. The integer n is not divisible by 12. Therefore, n is not divisible by 3.

   c) If n is an integer divisible by 3, then n is odd. The integer n is even. Therefore, n is not divisible by 3.

   d) If n is less than or equal to 4 and m is less than or equal to 3, then $n + m$ is less than or equal to 7. $n + m$ is greater than 7. Therefore, n is greater than 4 and m is greater than 3.

   e) If n is a prime number, then n is not divisible by 2. If n is not divisible by 2, then n is not even. n is an odd number. Therefore, n is a prime number.

2. Prove the following inferences:

   a)
   $$\begin{array}{l} p \rightarrow \sim q \\ r \leftrightarrow q \\ r \\ \hline \therefore \sim p \end{array}$$

b) $p \rightarrow q$

$\underline{p \wedge r}$

$\therefore q$

c) p

r

$\underline{(q \veebar p) \rightarrow \sim r}$

$\therefore q$

d) $p \rightarrow q$

$\underline{r \rightarrow \sim q}$

$\therefore r \rightarrow \sim p$

MATHEMATICAL PROOFS

If we want to proof that a given conditional, let us say:

$$P \rightarrow Q$$

is in fact a theorem, this is that it constitutes an implication, we must verify that the situation *P* true and *Q* false is never possible.

We can start the analysis from either P or Q. If we start from P, we will be following what is called the *direct proof method*. If we start from Q, we will be following the *indirect proof method.*

In general, the process is to chain from an initial proposition a series of true propositions, whose truths have been previously proven, until we get to prove the truth of the final proposition.

The direct proof method

To apply this method, we must start from *P*.

Let us recall the truth table of an implication. This is:

P	Q	$P \Rightarrow Q$
T	T	T
F	T	T
F	F	T

We can observe that when P is false, then Q can be either true or false (see the second and third row in the table). Therefore, this possibility does not require to be proved. Consequently, the attention must be focused on the combination given in the first row. This is, by starting from the truth of the antecedent, we must establish the truth of the consequent.

The process can be represented schematically as follows:

$$\begin{array}{l} P \\ P \Rightarrow P_1 \\ P_1 \Rightarrow P_2 \\ P_2 \Rightarrow P_3 \\ \vdots \\ P_n \Rightarrow Q \\ \hline \therefore Q \end{array}$$

Where $P_1, P_2, P_3, \cdots, P_n$ represent the propositions whose truth has been previously proved.

By observing the schematic representation, we realize that the direct proof method is a valid reasoning supported by the Hypothetical Syllogism and the Modus Ponendo Ponens. The chaining of propositions from *P* until *Q* is a successive application of SH that in a summarized way can be represented as follows:

$$P$$
$$P \Rightarrow Q$$

Then, according to MPP, the above is valid reasoning.

Example

By following the direct method, let us prove the theorem:

"If a, b and c are natural numbers such that a is a divisor of b and b is a divisor of c, then a is a divisor of c."

Let us use the symbol " | " to denote that a number is a divisor of another so that if we write "$x \mid y$", this can be read as "x is a divisor of y".

Thus, what we have to proof is the following implication:

$$[(a \mid b) \wedge (b \mid c)] \Rightarrow a \mid c$$

According to the direct proof method, we must start by accepting the truth of the antecedent, which in this case is the following:

$$(a \mid b) \wedge (b \mid c)$$

Then, we chain a series of propositions that we know are true either by definition or because they have been previously proved. We keep on doing this until proving the truth of the consequent.

We are going to explain the procedure step by step first and later we will present a schematic summary which makes the procedure shorter and easier to follow. Thus, we know that:

$$a \mid b \Rightarrow b = a \,.\, a' \quad (a' \text{ is a natural number}) \tag{1}$$

$$b \mid c \Rightarrow c = b \,.\, b' \quad (b' \text{ is a natural number}) \tag{2}$$

By replacing (1) in (2) we get

$$c = (a \,.\, a') \,.\, b' \tag{3}$$

By applying the associative property of multiplication in (3) we get

$$c = a \,.\, (a' \,.\, b') \tag{4}$$

Since a' and b' are both natural numbers, their product is also a natural number which we can call c' and replace it in (4). This is

$$c' = a' \,.\, b' \tag{5}$$

Replacing (5) in (4) leads to

$$c = a \,.\, c' \tag{6}$$

Thus, since c' is a natural number, we get that

$$c = a \,.\, c' \Rightarrow a \mid c$$

This is what we wanted to prove.

In summary, by accepting the truth of

$$(a \mid b) \wedge (b \mid c)$$

we have proven the truth of

$$a \mid c$$

by applying definitions and properties previously proven.

The procedure that we have followed above can be schematically represented as follows:

$(a \mid b) \wedge (b \mid c)$

$[(a \mid b) \wedge (b \mid c)]$	$\Rightarrow (b = a \,.\, a') \wedge (c = b \,.\, b')$	by definition, being a' and b' natural numbers
$[(b = a \,.\, a') \wedge (c = b \,.\, b')]$	$\Rightarrow [c = (a \,.\, a') \,.\, b']$	substitution of b
$[c = (a \,.\, a') \,.\, b']$	$\Rightarrow [c = a \,.\, (a' \,.\, b')]$	associative property
$[c = a \,.\, (a' \,.\, b')]$	$\Rightarrow c = a \,.\, c'$	being $c' = a' \,.\, b'$ natural number
$(c = a \,.\, c')$	$\Rightarrow (a \mid c)$	by definition

$\therefore a \mid c$

Students may use any of the forms presented above to proceed with a mathematical demonstration provided that each step in the chain of propositions is well justified.

The indirect proof method

Let us assume again that we want to prove that the conditional

$$P \rightarrow Q$$

is a theorem.

As we said earlier, to apply the indirect proof method we must start from the proposition Q. Let us recall one more time the truth table of an implication:

P	Q	$P \Rightarrow Q$
T	T	T
F	T	T
F	F	T

If Q is true, the antecedent P may be either true or false as it is shown by the two first rows of the table. Therefore, these two cases do not need a demonstration. However, if Q is false, then P must be also false for the conditional to be true (third row of the table). This is the case that must be proved. Thus, applying the indirect method requires that by starting from the assumption that Q is false we must prove that P is also false. Notice that this is equivalent to proving that the conditional

$$\sim Q \rightarrow \sim P$$

is an implication. This equivalence should not surprise us, since we learned earlier that

$$(P \rightarrow Q) \equiv (\sim Q \rightarrow \sim P)$$

This shows that both methods are equivalent. Therefore, the procedure is, in essence, the same. Schematically, it looks as follows:

$$\begin{array}{l} \sim Q \\ \sim Q \Rightarrow Q_1 \\ \quad Q_1 \Rightarrow Q_2 \\ \quad Q_2 \Rightarrow Q_3 \\ \quad \vdots \\ \quad Q_n \Rightarrow \sim P \\ \hline \therefore \sim P \end{array}$$

Examples

1. Let us prove the following theorem by following the indirect method:

   "If a, b, and c are naturals numbers such that $a + c$ is less than $b + c$, then a is less than b."

   The relationship "less than" is denoted by the symbol " $<$ ". Thus, we must prove that

   $$(a + c < b + c) \Rightarrow (a < b)$$

According to the indirect proof method, we must start by stating that the consequent is false and end up proving that the antecedent is also false.

The negation of the relationship "less than" is "greater than or equal to", which is denoted by the symbol "≥". This is:

$$\sim (a < b) \equiv a \geq b$$

Then we must start by stating that it is true that:

$$a \geq b$$

This is a very easy and short demonstration since we know that axiomatically if $a \geq b$ and c is any natural number, then it is true that

$$a + c \geq \mathrm{b} + c$$

This denies the antecedent of the given conditional which proves that it constitutes a theorem.

Schematically the demonstration is summarized as follows:

$a \geq b$

$(a \geq b) \Rightarrow (a + c \geq b + c)$ by axiom, being c any natural number

---

$\therefore a + c \geq b + c$

We applied the equivalence:

$$[(a + c < b + c) \Rightarrow (a < b)] \equiv [\sim (a < b) \Rightarrow \sim (a + c < b + c)]$$

$$\equiv [(a \geq b) \Rightarrow (a + c \geq b + c)]$$

2. Let us now consider the following theorem:

"Being a an integer, if a^2 is odd, then a is odd"

According to the indirect proof method, and by following the same reasoning as in the previous example, we should start from:

"a is even."

This means that being k an integer, we can write:

$$a = 2k \tag{1}$$

Therefore

$$a^2 = (2k)^2 \tag{2}$$

From (2) we get

$$a^2 = 4k^2 \tag{3}$$

By applying the Associative Property of multiplication in (3) we get

$$a^2 = 2(2k^2) \tag{4}$$

Being k an integer, then $2k.k = 2k^2$ is also integer which we call k'. Thus in (4) we have

$$a^2 = 2k'$$

This means that a^2 is even. The summary is as follows:

a is even		
a is even	$\Rightarrow a = 2k$	by definition, k integer
$a = 2k$	$\Rightarrow a^2 = (2k)^2$	
$a^2 = (2k)^2$	$\Rightarrow a^2 = 4k^2$	
$a^2 = 4k^2$	$\Rightarrow a^2 = 2(2k^2)$	associative property
$a^2 = 2(2k^2)$	$\Rightarrow a^2 = 2k'$	k' integer such that $k' = 2k.k = 2k^2$
$a^2 = 2k'$	$\Rightarrow a^2$ is even	by definition

$\therefore a^2$ is even

Notice that we have proved that

$$a \text{ is even} \Rightarrow a^2 \text{ is even}$$

As we saw earlier, this implication is equivalent to

$$\sim (a^2 \text{ is even}) \Rightarrow \sim (a \text{ is even})$$

Which in turn is equivalent to

$$a^2 \text{ is odd} \Rightarrow a \text{ is odd}$$

This is the given theorem that we wanted to prove.

The method of proof by contradiction

As before, let us assume that we want to proof that the conditional

$$P \rightarrow Q$$

is an implication. In other words, that it is a theorem. Once again, let us recall the truth table of the conditional. This is

p	q	$p \rightarrow q$
T	**T**	T
T	**F**	F
F	**T**	T
F	**F**	T

We have already seen that for the conditional to constitute an implication the combination of truth values in the second row cannot happen, since this is the only combination that makes the conditional false.

The method of *proof by contradiction*, also known as *reduction to absurdity* (from Latin *reduction ad absurdum*), focuses on proving that this combination is not possible.

The procedure is equivalent to try proving that the given conditional may not be an implication, which means that Q might be false while P is true. This is, that the conjunction

$$\sim Q \wedge P$$

may be true.

Therefore, the procedure must start by assuming that this conjunction is true. Then, if during the procedure of chaining propositions, we get any contradiction like this:

$$R \wedge \sim R$$

being *R* can any proposition, then this means that we have proved that

$$(\sim Q \wedge P) \Rightarrow (R \wedge \sim R)$$

This implication is confirming that the conjunction $\sim Q \wedge P$ is always false which in turn proves that the given conditional is always true. This is that in fact:

$$P \Rightarrow Q$$

what we wanted to prove.

The proof by contradiction is very useful in mathematics especially when we need to prove theorems whose demonstrations by applying either the direct or indirect method are very difficult, sometimes impossible.

This method can be summarized as follows:

> The *proof by contradiction or reduction to absurdity method* consists in assuming that the consequent of a given conditional is false being its antecedent true. Thus, if the procedure of chaining propositions leads to a contradiction, then this proves that the given conditional is in fact a theorem.

Example

Let us prove that the following conditional is a theorem:

"If m and n are both integer, such that $m.n$ is odd, then m and n are both odd."

Identifying the propositions as follows:

p: $m.n$ is odd.
Q: m and n are both odd

Then, we need to prove that

$$p \Rightarrow Q$$

To apply the proof by contradiction method we must start from

$$\sim Q \wedge p$$

This is:

"m and n are not both odd and $m.n$ is odd."

Therefore, if we assume that m and n are not both odd, means that at least one of them is not odd. Then, let us assume that n is even. Thus, being k an integer, we can write:

$$n = 2k$$

The product of m and n is

$$m.n = m(2k)$$

Applying both commutative and associative properties of multiplication we can rewrite this product as follows:

$$m.n = 2(km)$$

Since both k and m are integers, then their product is also an integer which we call k'. Therefore

$$m.n = 2k'$$

This means that $m.n$ is even, which contradicts the initial assumption that $m.n$ was odd. This contradiction proves that in fact:

$$p \Rightarrow Q$$

The reasoning explained above step by step can be schematically summarized as follows:

$\sim$ (m and n are both odd) $\wedge$
($m.n$ is odd)

[(m and n are **not** both odd) $\wedge$
($m.n$ is odd)] $\Rightarrow n$ is even

n is even	$\Rightarrow n = 2k$	by definition, k integer
$n = 2k$	$\Rightarrow m.n = m(2k)$	
$m.n = m(2k)$	$\Rightarrow m.n = 2(km)$	by commutative and associative properties
$m.n = 2(km)$	$\Rightarrow m.n = 2k'$	k' integer such that $k' = km$
$m.n = 2k'$	$\Rightarrow m.n$ is even	by definition

$\therefore$ ($m.n$ is even) $\wedge$ ($m.n$ is odd)

The conclusion is a contradiction what proves that the original conditional is in fact a theorem.

Proof by counterexample

The counterexample method is used to prove that a given conditional is not a theorem. Let us see how it works. Given the following conditional:

$$P \rightarrow Q$$

The method consists of finding at least one combination of true antecedent and a false consequent. In this situation, the conditional is false which means that it is not an implication.

Example

Given the following conditional:

"If n is an integer that is divisible by both 6 and 4, then n is divisible by 24."

The symbolic representation of this conditional is as follows:

$$[(6 \mid n) \wedge (4 \mid n)] \rightarrow (24 \mid n)$$

If we use the example of $n = 12$, which is divisible by both 6 and 4, we can verify that 12 is not divisible by 24. This is, the integer 12 is a counterexample because it makes the antecedent true, but the consequent false. Therefore, the given conditional is not a theorem.

EXERCISES IV

1. By applying the methods of mathematical proofs, determine if p is a sufficient, necessary, or necessary and sufficient condition for q in the following cases:

   a) p: $n + m$ is even and n is odd
   q: m is odd

   b) p: $n + m$ is even and n is even
   q: m is even

   c) p: $n \,.\, m$ is even
   q: n and m are both even

   d) p: n is an integer less than 2 and m is an integer less than 3
   q: $n \,.\, m$ is an integer less than 6

   e) p: a^2 is odd
   q: a is odd

f) *p*: *a* is an integer positive and *b* is an integer negative
q: *a*/*b* is an integer negative

g) *p*: *n* is an integer divisible by 4
q: *n* is an integer divisible by 2

h) *p*: $n^2 = 9$
q: $n = 3$

i) *p*: *a* is even
q: *a* ends in 6

j) *p*: *n* is an integer that ends in 5
q: *n* is an integer divisible by 5

k) *p*: *a* is divisible by 5
q: *a* is odd

l) *p*: $n + m$ is odd and *n* is even
q: *m* is odd

m) *p*: *n* is an integer divisible by 6
q: *n* is an integer divisible by 3

n) *p*: $n\ .\ m$ is even and *n* is odd
q: *m* is even

2. Prove whether the following conditionals are theorems or not:

   a) If *n* is less than 3 and *m* is less than 6, then *n.m* is less than 20 (*n* and *m* are both integer).

   b) If *n.m* and *n* are both odd, then *m* is odd.

   c) If *a* and *b* are both even, then $a + b$ is even.

d) If $n.m$ is less than or equal to 22, then n is less than or equal to 5 and m is less than or equal to 4 (n and m are integers).

e) If n is less than or equal to 5 and m is less than or equal to 4, then $n.m$ is less than or equal to 22 (n and m are natural numbers).

f) If $n.m$ is less than 20, then n is less than 3 and m is less than 6 (m and n are integers).

3. Prove that the following conditionals are theorems:

a) If x and y are both real numbers others than zero, then $x.y$ is a real number other than zero.

b) If a and b are both odd, then $a.b$ is odd.

c) If x is a real number other than zero, then x^{-1} is a real number other than zero.

d) If a^2 is even, then a is even.

e) $\sqrt{2}$ is an irrational number.

f) For all c positive, if $a + c$ is less than or equal to $b + c$, then a is less than or equal to b (a, b, and c are real numbers).

g) If n is an integer greater than 5, then $3n - 10$ is greater than 5.

h) If a is a natural number less than 2, then $2a + 3$ is less than 7.

i) If a is even and b is odd, then $a.b$ is even.

j) If a is odd and b is even, then $a + b$ is odd.

k) If a and b are both odd, then $a + b$ is even.

ANSWERS TO THE EXCERSICES PROPOSED IN CHAPTER 1

EXERCISES I

1. *a)* It is not *b)* $p \rightarrow q$ *c)* It is not *d)* $p \wedge q \wedge r$
   e) $p \rightarrow (q \wedge r)$ *f)* It is not *g)* p *h)* It is not
   i) $(p \wedge q) \rightarrow r$ *j)* $p \rightarrow (q \veebar r)$

2.
   a) If inflation hurts people with fixed income, then it destroys the purchasing power.
   b) If inflation hurts people with fixed income and destroys the purchasing power, then the less the government's expenses the lower the risk of inflation.
   c) The less the government's expenses the lower the risk of inflation or it destroys the purchasing power and hurts people with fixed income.
   d) If inflation does not destroy the purchasing power, then the less the government's expenses the lower the risk of inflation and it does not hurt people with fixed income.
   e) Either it is not true that the less the government's expenses the lower the risk of inflation or inflation hurts people with fixed income and destroys the purchasing power.
   f) It is not true that inflation hurts people with fixed income and destroys the purchasing power.
   g) Inflation hurts people with fixed income if and only if destroys the purchasing power and the less the government's expenses the lower the risk of inflation.
   h) It is not true that if inflation hurts people with fixed income, then either it destroys the purchasing power or the less the government's expenses the lower the risk of inflation.

3.

a) $\sim[(p \wedge \sim q) \rightarrow \sim r]$ *b)* $r \rightarrow \sim(\sim q \veebar p)$

4.

a) $\sim(p \vee q)$ *b)* $\sim(p \wedge q)$

c) $\sim(p \rightarrow q)$ or $(p \wedge \sim q)$ or $(\sim p \vee \sim q)$

5.

a) $(p \wedge q) \rightarrow r$, is T *b)* $p \wedge (q \rightarrow r)$, is T

c) $(p \wedge q) \rightarrow (r \veebar s)$, is T *d)* $p \veebar (q \wedge r)$, is T

e) $(p \wedge q) \rightarrow r$, is T

6. *a)* F *b)* T *c)* T

7. *a)* Yes *b)* Yes *c)* Yes *d)* No *e)* No *f)* Yes

8. *a)* $p \veebar q$ *b)* $[(p \wedge q) \rightarrow r] \wedge (\sim p \rightarrow r)$ *c)* $p \rightarrow (q \wedge r)$

9. *a)* Either T or F *b)* Either T or F *c) T* *d)* Either T or F *e)* T

10.

11. *a)* T *b)* T *c)* T *d)* T *e)* T *f)* T

12. *a)* Yes *b)* Yes *c)* No *d)* No *e)* Yes

f) Yes *g)* No *h)* Yes *i)* No j*)* No

13. *a)* Ind *b)* Ind *c)* Ind *d)* Ind *e)* Ind *f)* Taut *g)* Ind *h)* Ind *i)* Ind *j)* Ind *k)* Ind *l)* Ind *m)* Ind

14. *a)* No *b)* Yes *c)* No *d)* Yes *e)* Yes *f)* Yes *g)* Yes *h)* No

EXERCISES II

1.

a)

Converse: If $a - b$ is even, then a and b are both odd.
Inverse: If a or b is even, then $a - b$ is odd.
Contrapositive: If $a - b$ is odd, then a or b is even.

b)

Converse: If the living cost increases with inflation, then inflation destroys the purchasing power.
Inverse: If inflation does not destroy the purchasing power, then the living cost does not increase with inflation.
Contrapositive: If the living cost does not increase with inflation, then inflation does not destroy the purchasing power.

c)

Converse: If n is divisible by 9, the n is divisible by 3.
Inverse: If n is not divisible by 3, then n is not divisible by 9.
Contrapositive: If n is not divisible by 9, the n is not divisible by 3.

d)

Converse: If the balance of payments of a country is negative, then its exports are greater than its imports.
Inverse: If a country's exports are less than its imports, then its balance of payments is positive.
Contrapositive: If the balance of payments of a country is positive, then its exports are less than its imports.

e)

Converse: If wages in the same type of job are the same, then the labor market is perfectly competitive.
Inverse: If the labor market is not perfectly competitive, then wages in the same type of job are different.
Contrapositive: If wages in the same type of job are different, then the labor market is not perfectly competitive.

f)

Converse: If an integer number ends in 5, then it is divisible by 5.

Inverse: If an integer number is not divisible by 5, then it does not end in 5.

Contrapositive: If an integer number does not end in 5, then it is not divisible by 5.

g)

Converse: If ABC is an equilateral triangle, then ABC is an isosceles triangle .

Inverse: If ABC is not an isosceles triangle, then ABC is not an equilateral triangle

Contrapositive: If ABC is not an equilateral triangle, then ABC is not an isosceles triangle

h)

Converse: If a is an even number, then a^2 is even.

Inverse: If a^2 is not an even number, then a is not even.

Contrapositive: If a is not an even number, then a^2 is not even.

i)

Converse: If his expenses are less than his income, then his net savings are positive, and his assets increase.

Inverse: If his net savings are negative or his assets decrease, then his expenses are greater than his income.

Contrapositive: If his expenses are greater than his income, then his net savings are negative, or his assets decrease.

2.

a) Statement: T, Converse: F, Inverse: F, Contrapositive: T
b) Statement: F, Converse: T, Inverse: T, Contrapositive: F
c) Statement: T, Converse: F, Inverse: F, Contrapositive: T
d) Statement: T, Converse: F, Inverse: F, Contrapositive: T

EXERCISES III

1.

a)
$$\begin{array}{l} p \to q \\ q \to r \\ \underline{\sim r} \\ \therefore \sim p \end{array}$$
(Valid)

b)
$$\begin{array}{l} p \to q \\ q \to r \\ \underline{\sim p} \\ \therefore \sim r \end{array}$$
(Not valid)

c)
$$\begin{array}{l} p \to q \\ \underline{\sim q} \\ \therefore \sim p \end{array}$$
(Valid)

a)
$$\begin{array}{l} (p \wedge q) \to r \\ \underline{\sim r} \\ \therefore \sim p \wedge \sim q \end{array}$$
(Not valid)

e)
$$\begin{array}{l} p \to \sim q \\ \sim q \to \sim r \\ \underline{\sim r} \\ \therefore p \end{array}$$
(Not valid)

EXERCISES IV

1.

a) Sufficient *b)* Sufficient *c)* Necessary *d)* None
e) Necessary and sufficient *f)* Sufficient *g)* Sufficient
h) Necessary *i)* Necessary *j)* Sufficient *k)* None
l) Sufficient *m)* Sufficient *n)* Sufficient

2.

a) No *b)* Yes *c)* Yes *d)* No
e) Yes *f)* No

Chapter 2: Set Theory

This chapter is devoted to introducing set theory whose concepts support the formal definition of many fundamental concepts of Calculus. Set theory is regarded as a branch of mathematical logic. Therefore, we will see how the concepts learned in the previous chapter are used to developing the body of concepts and the language of set theory which in turn are used in the definitions of many fundamental concepts of Calculus.

Set theory is built based on intuitive and understandable concepts that do not need formal definitions. In the real world, there are "things", "objects", "entities", "elements" which constitute fully identifiable units that can be either tangible or not. These "elements" can be grouped according to some criterion forming what we call a set. Therefore, we say that elements are members of sets. Thus, set theory is developed upon the base of these three basic concepts: element, membership, and set.

Although we do not provide formal definitions for the three basic concepts mentioned above, they must be fully identifiable to allow a formal theoretical development. Thus, an appropriate system of representation and identification must be available.

NOTATION

Sets are usually denoted by capital letters such as A, B, C, D, etc., while their elements or members are denoted by small letters such as a, b, c, d, etc. Sets that have a finite number of elements may be described by listing all their elements enclosed in curly braces. For example, if A is the set of the first five natural numbers, we may write:

$$\mathbf{A} = \{1, 2, 3, 4, 5\}$$

To denote the membership relation between sets and their elements, we use the symbol $\in$. Thus, to denote that an element a is a member of the set A we write:

$$a \in \mathbf{A}$$

This can be read by using any of the following expressions:

"*a* is a member of ***A***"	or
"*a* is an element of ***A***"	or
"*a* is in ***A***"	or
"*a* belongs to ***A***"	or
"*a* lie in ***A***"	

The negation of the membership relation is denoted by $\notin$ such that we can write:

$$a \notin \mathbf{A}$$

And it is read by using the negation of the expressions given earlier. These are:

"*a* is not a member of ***A***"	or
"*a* is not an element of ***A***"	or
"*a* is not in ***A***"	or
"*a* does not belong to ***A***"	or
"*a* does not lie in ***A***"	

When defining a particular set, it is advisable to consider the following:

1) A set must be defined unambiguously. This allows determining without a doubt whether a particular element is a member of that set.

2) The elements of a given set must be different from one another. No element can be repeated. If this happens, it is counted only once.

3) The order in which the elements are written in a set does not matter. Changing the order in which the elements are written does not imply that the given set changes.

SET OF SETS

There are sets whose elements are all sets. These sets are called "set of sets". For example, let us say that sets ***A***, ***B***, ***C***, and ***D*** in turn form another set ***P***. In this case, we can write:

$$\mathbf{P} = \{\mathbf{A}, \mathbf{B}, \mathbf{C}, \mathbf{D}\}$$

A set of sets is the only case in which its elements are denoted by capital letters since they are themselves sets. Sometimes we need to write each of the sets that form another set by explicitly listing all their elements. For example, let us say that we have the following sets:

$$\mathbf{A} = \{a, b, c\} \qquad \mathbf{B} = \{1, 2, 3, 4\} \qquad \mathbf{C} = \{r, s, t\}$$

Suppose that A, B, and C constitute a set P. If for any reason we need to write P by listing all the elements of A, B, and C, then we can write P as follows:

$$\mathbf{P} = \{\{a, b, c\}, \{1, 2, 3, 4\}, \{r, s, t\}\}$$

DESCRIBING SETS

In general, there are two ways of describing a set. One is by listing or enumerating all its elements and enclosing them in curly braces as we have done it in the examples given above. This way is known as a *description by extension* or *extensional definition* of a set. This method is also known as the *roster method.* It can be used only when the set contains a finite number of elements as far as this is a small number so that it is possible to write each element.

Another way to describe a set is by *comprehension* also known as an *intentional definition* or *set-builder notation*. This way consists of writing and enclosing in curly braces a property or properties that characterize its members, and only them, so that we can unequivocally establish whether a given element is a member of that set or not. For example,

$$\mathbf{A} = \{\text{Natural numbers less than 50 and multiples of both 3 and 5}\}$$

This set is

$$\mathbf{A} = \{15, 30, 45\}$$

In this example it is possible to describe the set A using both ways. However, when the number of members is infinite it is only possible to describe the set by comprehension, this is using the set-builder notation. In these cases, using symbols to describe the sets is very helpful. Many of these symbols are the same symbols that have already been introduced in Chapter 1 as well as other symbols known as *quantifiers* that will be introduced later. For example, in the case of the set A described earlier, instead of writing a long statement by using words, we can simplify its description by writing

$$\mathbf{A} = \{x : x \in N \wedge x < 50 \wedge 3 \mid x \wedge 5 \mid x\}$$

Where the *colon* symbol " : " is read as "such that" and N represents the set of natural numbers.

In what follows in this chapter we will be working on definitions of concepts, properties, theorems, and proofs for which we need a general description of sets given by comprehension, this is, by using the set-builder notation. For this purpose, we use the symbol $P(x)$ to represent the property, statement, or predicate that defines a general set applied to an indeterminate element x. For example, let us assume that we want to refer to the set of even numbers. Then we can write

$$p(x): x \text{ is even.}$$

You may recall from Chapter 1 that the statement "x is even" is not a proposition itself. It will become a proposition when we assign a specific value to x. Therefore, for each value given to x, we get a different proposition so that we can state whether $p(x)$ is true or false. In the given example we may have

$$p(4): 4 \text{ is even} \quad (T)$$
$$p(7): 7 \text{ is even} \quad (F)$$

Therefore, when we write

$$\mathbf{A} = \{x: P(x)\}$$

We are stating that A is the set of elements that satisfy (make true) the property, general statement, or predicate denoted by $P(x)$.

Thus, for any given element a we can state that

$$a \in A \Leftrightarrow P(a) \text{ is T}$$
$$a \notin A \Leftrightarrow P(a) \text{ is F}$$

In the following example given earlier:

$$\mathbf{A} = \{x: x \in N \wedge x < 50 \wedge 3 \mid x \wedge 5 \mid x\}$$

We have that the statement $P(x)$ is

$$P(x): x \in N \wedge x < 50 \wedge 3 \mid x \wedge 5 \mid x$$

Thus, we can state that $30 \in A$ because $P(30)$ is T, while $10 \notin A$ because $P(10)$ is F.

We can see that propositions play an important role in the definitions of sets. In general, propositional logic provides fundamental support in developing the set theory. There is a clear equivalence between the languages of both the set theory and propositional logic. The laws of logic are applied in the formulation of definitions, properties, and theorems that constitute the set theory.

QUANTIFIERS

Quantifiers are symbols used to express the quantity of elements members of a certain set that make a given property or relation true. There are two types of quantifiers: universal and existential.

Universal quantifier

The universal quantifier is used to express that *all members* of a certain set satisfy a given property or relation. This quantifier is denoted by the symbol ∀ (an inverted **A**) which can be read as "for all".

Thus, if we want to express that all members of a set ***A*** satisfy a given property *P(x)*, then by sing the universal quantifier we can write

$$\forall x \in \mathbf{A}: P(x)$$

This means that applying *P(x)* to each member of the set ***A*** we get a resulting proposition that is true. Therefore, the conjunction of all those propositions is also true. Thus, if the set ***A*** is such that

$$\mathbf{A} = \{x_1, x_2, \cdots, x_n\}$$

The following equivalence is verified:

$$[\forall x \in A: P(x)] \equiv [P(x_1) \wedge P(x_2) \wedge \cdots \wedge P(x_n)]$$

If we want to express the opposite, this is, that *no element* of another set, let us say ***B***, satisfies the property *P(x)*, then we can write

$$\forall x \in \mathbf{B}: \sim P(x)$$

In other words, the above statement means that all members of the set ***B*** make *P(x)* false.

Existential quantifier

While the universal quantifier refers to all members of a given set, the existential quantifier is used to express that *at least one* of them satisfies a given property. The symbol to represent the existential quantifier looks like a flipped E. This is ∃ which is usually read as "there exists at least one", but it also can be read as "there exists" or "for some". Therefore, when we write

$$\exists\, x \in \mathbf{A}\colon P(x)$$

It means that there is at least one member of the set ***A*** that makes the property *P(x)* true. In other words, when applying the property *P(x)* to each member of ***A*** at least one of the resulting propositions is true. Therefore, the inclusive disjunction of all those propositions is also be true. Thus, in the case of a set ***A*** such that

$$\mathbf{A} = \{x_1, x_2, \cdots, x_n\}$$

The following equivalence is verified:

$$[\exists\, x \in A\colon P(x)] \equiv [P(x_1) \vee P(x_2) \vee \cdots \vee P(x_n)]$$

If we want to express that no element of ***A*** satisfies some other property, let us say *Q(x)*, we use the symbol ∄ which can be read as "there is not" or "no element" or "for no", etc. Thus, we can write

$$\nexists\, x \in A\colon Q(x)$$

In this case we can read the whole statement as follows: "there is not *x* in the set ***A*** that makes *Q(x)* true" which is the same as: "no element in ***A*** satisfies *Q(x)*".

Notice that the following equivalences are verified:

$$[\nexists\, x \in \mathbf{A}: Q(x)] \equiv [\forall x \in \mathbf{A}: \sim Q(x)] \equiv \sim [\exists\, x \in \mathbf{A}: Q(x)]$$

Likewise, the following equivalence is verified:

$$\sim [\forall x \in \mathbf{A}: Q(x)] \equiv [\exists\, x \in \mathbf{A}: \sim Q(x)]$$

These equivalences show that the negation of the universal quantifier can be expressed in terms of the existential quantifier and vice versa. It will also be useful to know that

$$[\forall x \in \mathbf{A}: P(x)] \Rightarrow [\exists\, x \in \mathbf{A}: P(x)]$$

However, the converse is not true. This is:

$$[\exists\, x \in \mathbf{A}: P(x)] \nRightarrow [\forall x \in \mathbf{A}: P(x)]$$

Where the symbol $\nRightarrow$ is read as "does not imply"

THE UNIVERSAL SET

The universal set is the set that contains all the elements of a given situation of interest. This set establishes the reference, the context, or the frontiers within which we are working. It is also known as the referential set.

For example, let us suppose that we want to conduct statistical research on education. We can establish the context of our work to the limits of Harvard University. However, we could be interested in extending the study to all universities in the United States.

As we can see, the universal set is not unique. The delimitation depends on the objective of the specific work or research we are conducting.

The most usual notation of the universal set is the capital letter ***U***. However, sometimes we can find that the universal set is also denoted by the Greek letter **Ω**.

By using the language that we learned in the previous chapter on propositional logic, we can provide a formal definition for the universal set. Let us assume that ***A*** is a given set such that

$$\mathbf{A} = \{x\text{: } P(x)\}$$

Since the universal set has been defined as the set that contains all the elements of a given situation of interest, this implies that it is formed by the elements that are members of ***A*** and also by the elements that are not members of ***A*** within the frontiers of the given situation. In other words, the universal set of this situation is constituted by those elements that make *P(x)* true, and by those that make it false. Therefore, if we want to describe the universal set of this situation by comprehension, we can write

$$\mathbf{U} = \{x\text{: } P(x) \vee \sim P(x)\}$$

Thus, any element x within the frontiers of the established situation makes the inclusive disjunction $P(x) \vee \sim P(x)$ true. Since this disjunction will always be true within the established frontiers, the universal set is thus defined by a tautology.

THE EMPTY SET

The set having no elements is called the empty set. This is a unique set that is usually denoted by the symbol ∅. Since this set has no elements, any statement that is not true for all elements within a given situation is suitable to define the empty set. This is the case of the following contradiction:

$$P(x) \wedge \sim P(x)$$

Therefore

$$\varnothing = \{x: P(x) \wedge \sim P(x)\}$$

Any contradiction is suitable to define the empty set.

The fact that the empty set is unique means that it is the same in any situation. This will be formally proven later.

Example

Let us have the set ***A*** such that

$$\mathbf{A} = \{x: x \in \boldsymbol{Z} \wedge 7x - 3 = 0\}$$

Z represents the set of integer numbers.

We can easily verify that there is not any integer number that satisfies the equation $7x - 3 = 0$. Therefore, we conclude that

$$\nexists\, x \in \boldsymbol{Z}: 7x - 3 = 0$$

This implies that ***A*** has no elements and therefore

$$\mathbf{A} = \varnothing.$$

THE SINGLETON SET

We call *singleton* set to a set that contains exactly one element. This type of set is also known as a *unit set.*

Example

Let us have the set ***A*** such that

$$\boldsymbol{A} = \{x \colon x \in \boldsymbol{Z} \wedge x > 3 \wedge x < 5\}$$

There is only one integer that simultaneously satisfies that $x > 3$ and $x < 5$. This is $x = 4$.

Before proceeding it is important to point out that the most common way of writing the statement

$$x > 3 \wedge x < 5$$

is as follows:

$$3 < x < 5$$

In general, given two any numbers a and b such that $a < b$, the statement:

$$x > a \wedge x < b$$

is usually written as:

$$a < x < b$$

Returning to our example we have that

$$\mathbf{A} = \{x \colon x \in \boldsymbol{Z} \wedge x > 3 \wedge x < 5\} = \{x \colon x \in \boldsymbol{Z} \wedge 3 < x < 5\} = \{4\}$$

Therefore, $\boldsymbol{A}$ is a singleton set.

The definition of a singleton set allows us to highlight important differences between following notations:

$$a, \qquad \{a\} \qquad \text{and} \qquad \{\{a\}\}$$

The first one refers to the element a, the second one is the singleton set whose only member is the element a, and the third one denotes a singleton set of sets whose only element is in turn the singleton set $\{a\}$. Also notice that, for example

$$\mathbf{A} = \{a, a, a\} = \{a\}$$

$\boldsymbol{A}$ is a singleton set because its only element is a which has been written three times but, according to what we said earlier, it counts only once.

Also, if we had a set like the following:

$$\mathbf{A} = \{\{a, b, c\}\}$$

We say that *A* is a singleton set because it contains only one element which is a set that contains three elements.

To conclude this section, it is also important to point out that the empty set is not equal to the set contains only the empty set. This is

$$\varnothing \neq \{\varnothing\}$$

EXERCISES I

1. Determine by extension (roster method) the following sets:

   $\mathbf{A} = \{x: x = 2n - 1 \wedge n \in \boldsymbol{N}^* \wedge n \leq 5\}$
   $\boldsymbol{N}^*$: The set of natural numbers without zero.

   $\mathbf{B} = \{x: x = 2n \wedge n \in \boldsymbol{N}^* \wedge x \leq 10\}$

   $\mathbf{C} = \{x: x \in \boldsymbol{Z} \wedge -25 \leq x^3 \leq 50\}$; ***Z*:** The set of integer numbers.

   $\mathbf{D} = \{x: x = 2n + 1 \wedge n \in \boldsymbol{N}^* \wedge n \leq 9\}$

   $\mathbf{E} = \{x: x \in \boldsymbol{N} \wedge x^2 - 2x + 8 = 0\}$
   $\boldsymbol{N}$: The set of natural numbers including zero.

   $\mathbf{F} = \{x: x \in N^* \wedge x + 2 \leq 11\}$

2. State which of the following expressions are true. Justify your answers.

   a) $a \in \{\{a\}\}$ *b)* $\{a, b\} \in \{a, \{a, b\}\}$

   c) $\{a, \{a\}\} = \{a\}$ *d)* $\{a, b, c\} = \{a, c, a, b\}$

   e) $\{a, a, b, c\} \neq \{a, b, b, c\}$ *f)* $\{a, b, c\} = \{b, a, c\}$

3. Write in words the meaning of the following expressions:

   a) $\mathbf{A} = \{x: x \in \boldsymbol{N} \wedge x \leq 6\}$

   b) $\mathbf{B} = \{x: x \in \boldsymbol{Q} \wedge (x + ½) \in \boldsymbol{N}\}$; $\boldsymbol{Q}$: The set of rational numbers.

   c) $\mathbf{C} = \{x: x \in \boldsymbol{N} \wedge 5 \leq 4x - 6 \leq 30\}$

   d) Being a a straight line in the plane:
   $\mathbf{H} = \{r: r \text{ is a straight line} \wedge r \parallel a\}$

   e) Being a a straight line in the plane:
   $\mathbf{M} = \{r: r \text{ is a straight line} \wedge r \perp a\}$

   f) $\mathbf{E} = \{x: x \in \boldsymbol{N} \wedge 2 < 2x - 3 \leq 11\}$

   g) $\mathbf{F} = \{x: x \in \boldsymbol{N} \wedge x \notin \boldsymbol{E}\}$

4 Describe by comprehension, using set-builder notation, the following sets:

   a) The set of even natural numbers.

   b) The set of real solutions of the equation $x^3 - 2x^2 - x + 2 = 0$.

   c) The set of natural numbers that satisfy: $-16 < 10x - 78 \leq 3$.

5 Describe by comprehension, using set-builder notation, the following sets:

   a) $A = \{1, 3, 5, 7, 9, 11, 13, 15\}$

   b) $B = \{1, 4, 9, 16, 25, 36\}$

c) $C = \{1, 2, 3, 5, 7, 11, 13, 17, 19, 23\}$

d) $D = \{1, 2, 4, 8, 16, 32, 64\}$

6. Suppose that a is an element of the set $\boldsymbol{B}$ and $\boldsymbol{B}$ is an element of the set $\boldsymbol{C}$. Can we conclude that a is an element of the set $\boldsymbol{C}$? Explain.

7. Determine which of the following sets are empty:

   a) $A = \{x\text{: } x \text{ is odd and divisible by } 2\}$

   b) $B = \{x\text{: } x \in Z \wedge x + 3 = 3\}$

   c) $C = \{x\text{: } x \in \boldsymbol{R} \wedge x^2 = 10 \wedge 2x = 10\}$
   $\boldsymbol{R}$: The set of real numbers

   d) $D = \{\varnothing\}$

VENN DIAGRAMS

Venn Diagrams constitute a graphic system used to illustrate sets, their elements, operations, and logical relationships between them. They provide important help in understanding the concepts that we are going to see in the next pages. These diagrams are built according to the following criteria:

a) The universal set is represented by a rectangle containing all other sets referred to a given situation.

b) The sets within the situation are represented by circles.

c) When it is possible, the elements which are members of sets can be represented by dots inside the corresponding circle that represents the set, and then each dot is identified with the corresponding name, letter, or number.

Example

Let us represent the following sets by using Venn Diagrams:

A $= \{x: x \in N^* \wedge x < 5\}$ **B** $= \{x: x \in N^* \wedge 3 \leq x < 10\}$

C $= \{x: x \in N^* \wedge 3|x \wedge x \leq 9\}$ **D** $= \{x: x \in N^* \wedge 12|x \wedge x < 25\}$

We assume that the universal set is ***N***. Described by extension the given sets are:

$A = \{1, 2, 3, 4\}$ $B = \{3, 4, 5, 6, 7, 8, 9\}$

$C = \{3, 6, 9\}$ $D = \{12, 24\}$

The corresponding Venn diagram looks like this:

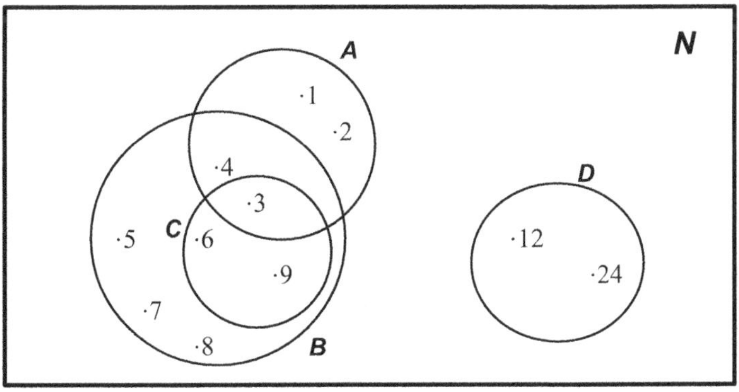

Figure 2.1

EQUALITY OF SETS

Given the sets ***A*** and ***B***, we say that they are equal if and only if they contain the same elements. Therefore, each element of ***A*** is also a member of ***B*** and vice versa. By using symbols, this is

$$(\mathbf{A} = \mathbf{B}) \Leftrightarrow (x \in \mathbf{A} \Rightarrow x \in \mathbf{B}) \wedge (x \in \mathbf{B} \Rightarrow x \in \mathbf{A})$$

Therefore

$$(\mathbf{A} = \mathbf{B}) \Leftrightarrow (x \in \mathbf{A} \Leftrightarrow x \in \mathbf{B})$$

Let us assume that ***A*** and ***B*** are both defined by comprehension by *P(x)* and *Q(x)* respectively, such that

$$\mathbf{A} = \{x: P(x)\} \qquad \text{and} \qquad \mathbf{B} = \{x: Q(x)\}$$

Also, assume that ***A*** = ***B***. Then, following the scheme applied for logical reasoning we can write

$$\begin{array}{ll} P(x) & \\ P(x) \Rightarrow x \in \mathbf{A} & \\ x \in \mathbf{A} \Rightarrow x \in \mathbf{B} & \text{Since } \mathbf{A} = \mathbf{B} \\ x \in \mathbf{B} \Rightarrow Q(x) & \\ \hline \therefore\ Q(x) & \end{array}$$

Therefore

$$P(x) \Rightarrow Q(x)$$

Likewise, we can prove that

$$Q(x) \Rightarrow P(x)$$

Thus, we have that

$$(\mathbf{A} = \mathbf{B}) \Leftrightarrow [P(x) \Leftrightarrow Q(x)] \equiv [P(x) \equiv Q(x)]$$

As a result, we get the following formal definition for equality of sets:

> Given the sets ***A*** and ***B*** such that
>
> $$\mathrm{A} = \{x: P(x)\} \qquad \mathrm{B} = \{x: Q(x)\}$$
>
> $$(\mathrm{A} = \mathrm{B}) \Leftrightarrow [P(x) \equiv Q(x)]$$

Example

Given the sets:

$$\mathbf{A} = \{x \colon x \in \boldsymbol{Z} \wedge x^2 \leq 4\}$$

$$\mathbf{B} = \{x \colon x \in \boldsymbol{Z} \wedge -2 \leq x \leq 2\}$$

Since

$$(x^2 \leq 4) \equiv (-2 \leq x \leq 2)$$

These sets are equals, and defined by extension they are

$$\mathbf{A} = \{-2, -1, 0, 1, 2\} = \mathbf{B}$$

We can see that they have the same elements.

Properties of equality of sets

Given the sets:

$$\mathbf{A} = \{x \colon P(x)\} \qquad \mathbf{B} = \{x \colon Q(x)\} \qquad \mathbf{C} = \{x \colon R(x)\}$$

The equality of sets satisfies the following properties:

1) *Identity*

$$\mathbf{A} = \mathbf{A}$$

Supported by the equivalence:

$$P(x) \equiv P(x)$$

2) *Commutativity*

$$(\mathbf{A} = \mathbf{B}) \equiv (\mathbf{B} = \mathbf{A})$$

Supported by

$$[P(x) \equiv Q(x)] \equiv [Q(x) \equiv P(x)]$$

3) *Transitivity*

$$(\mathbf{A} = \mathbf{B}) \wedge (\mathbf{B} = \mathbf{C}) \Rightarrow (\mathbf{A} = \mathbf{C})$$

Supported by

$$[P(x) \equiv Q(x)] \wedge [Q(x) \equiv R(x)] \Rightarrow [P(x) \equiv R(x)]$$

RELATION OF SET INCLUSION

Given the sets ***A*** and ***B***, if all elements in ***A*** are also members of ***B***, then we say that ***A*** is a *Subset* of ***B***. We can also say that ***A*** is *contained* in ***B***.

This relationship between ***A*** and ***B*** is called *inclusion*. To represent this relationship, we use the symbol ⊆ such that we can write

$$\mathbf{A} \subseteq \mathbf{B}$$

According to the given definition, it is verified that

$$(\mathbf{A} \subseteq \mathbf{B}) \Leftrightarrow (x \in \mathbf{A} \Rightarrow x \in \mathbf{B})$$

I the sets ***A*** and ***B*** are equal (***A*** = ***B***), the above definition is still satisfied.

If ***A*** and ***B*** are not equal, and ***A*** is a subset of ***B***, then we call this relationship *strict inclusion*, and ***A*** is identified as a *proper subset* of ***B***. In this case we use the symbol ⊂ and we write

$$\mathbf{A} \subset \mathbf{B}$$

This is

$$(\mathbf{A} \subset \mathbf{B}) \Leftrightarrow (\mathbf{A} \subseteq \mathbf{B} \wedge \mathbf{A} \neq \mathbf{B})$$

If the sets ***A*** and ***B*** are both defined by comprehension, we can state the following definition:

Given A and B such that

$$A = \{x: P(x)\} \quad B = \{x: Q(x)\}$$

$$(A \subseteq B) \Leftrightarrow [P(x) \Rightarrow Q(x)]$$

By applying the logical equivalence between an implication and its contrapositive form, the definition given above can also be written as

$$(\mathbf{A} \subseteq \mathbf{B}) \Leftrightarrow [\sim Q(x) \Rightarrow \sim P(x)]$$

This also means that

$$(\mathbf{A} \subseteq \mathbf{B}) \Leftrightarrow (x \notin \mathbf{B} \Rightarrow x \notin \mathbf{A})$$

By using Venn diagram, the set inclusion $A \subset B$ is illustrated in Figure 2.2.

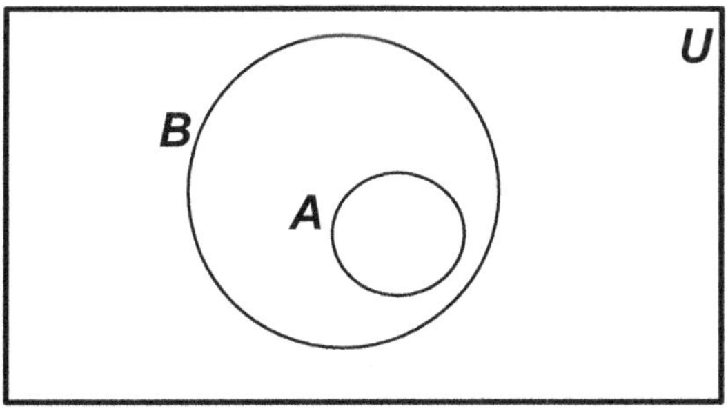

Figure 2.2

The previous Figure 2.1 shows the example $C \subset B$.

According to the definition of set inclusion, and supported by figures 2.1 and 2.2, it can be verified that every set is a subset of the universal set of a given situation.

Example

A good example of a strict inclusion relationship between sets is the one that satisfy the numerical sets ***N*** and ***Z***. Given that any natural number is also an integer, this means that

$$x \in \boldsymbol{N} \Rightarrow x \in \boldsymbol{Z}$$

and since the converse of that implication is not true, then they satisfy that

$$\boldsymbol{N} \subset \boldsymbol{Z}$$

By representing the set of rational and real numbers by the capital letters ***Q*** and ***R*** respectively, the following relationships are also satisfied:

$$\boldsymbol{Z} \subset \boldsymbol{Q} \subset \boldsymbol{R}$$

Properties of set inclusion

1) *Reflexive*

Any set is a subset of itself.

Let ***A*** be the set such that

$$\mathbf{A} = \{x\text{: } P(x)\}$$

Supported by the logical law

$$P(x) \Rightarrow P(x)$$

According to the definition, this implication means that

$$\mathbf{A} \subseteq \mathbf{A}$$

2) *Transitive*

Given the sets

$\mathbf{A} = \{x\text{: } P(x)\}$ $\qquad$ $\mathbf{B} = \{x\text{: } Q(x)\}$ $\qquad$ $\mathbf{C} = \{x\text{: } R(x)\}$

Then

$$[(\mathbf{A} \subseteq \mathbf{B}) \wedge (\mathbf{B} \subseteq \mathbf{C})] \Rightarrow (\mathbf{A} \subseteq \mathbf{C})$$

Proof:

In propositional language, this property is translated as

$$[P(x) \Rightarrow Q(x)] \wedge [Q(x) \Rightarrow R(x)] \Rightarrow [P(x) \Rightarrow R(x)]$$

We can verify that this implication is the Hypothetical Syllogism law which proves the transitive property.

3) *Antisymmetric*

$$[(\mathbf{A} \subseteq \mathbf{B}) \wedge (\mathbf{B} \subseteq \mathbf{A})] \Leftrightarrow (\mathbf{A} = \mathbf{B})$$

Proof:

In propositional language this property is

$$[P(x) \Rightarrow Q(x)] \wedge [Q(x) \Rightarrow P(x)] \Leftrightarrow [P(x) \equiv R(x)]$$

This is a logical law that involves the definition of both the double implication and logically equivalent propositions. This law proves the antisymmetric property.

Characteristics of the empty set

After having studied the relation of set inclusion, we can now establish two important characteristics of the empty set.

1) *The empty set is a subset of any other set*

Given a set A such that

$$\mathbf{A} = \{x\text{: } P(x)\}$$

Then

$$\varnothing \subseteq A$$

Proof:

Any element x that is not a member of A is not a member of $\varnothing$ either, since $\varnothing$ has no elements. This can be written as

$$x \notin A \Rightarrow x \notin \varnothing$$

The above is the definition of set inclusion given in terms of the contrapositive form of an implication. Therefore, it proves that

$$\varnothing \subseteq A$$

2) *The empty set is unique.*

Let us assume that there are two different empty sets, say $\varnothing$ and $\varnothing'$. According to the characteristic 1) proven above, since both $\varnothing$ and $\varnothing'$ are empty sets it is true that

$$\varnothing \subseteq \varnothing'$$

And it is also true that

$$\varnothing' \subseteq \varnothing$$

Therefore, according to the antisymmetric property

$$[\varnothing \subseteq \varnothing'] \wedge [\varnothing' \subseteq \varnothing] \Leftrightarrow [\varnothing = \varnothing']$$

This proves that the empty set is unique.

Complement of a subset

Given the sets $\boldsymbol{A}$ and $\boldsymbol{B}$ such that $\boldsymbol{A}$ is a subset of $\boldsymbol{B}$, *the complement of A respect to B* is the set of elements of $\boldsymbol{B}$ that are not elements of $\boldsymbol{A}$. To denote this set, we use the symbol $\mathbf{C}_{B}\boldsymbol{A}$. Thus, according to the definition, the complement of ***A*** respect to ***B*** is the following set:

$$\mathbf{C_B A} = \{x: x \in \boldsymbol{B} \wedge x \notin \boldsymbol{A}\}$$

In case that ***A*** and ***B*** are both defined by the statements *P(x)* and *Q(x)* respectively, the formal definition is as follows:

Given the sets *A* and *B* such as $A \subseteq B$ and

$$A = \{x: P(x)\} \quad \text{and} \quad B = \{x: Q(x)\}$$

The *complement of A respect to B* is the set denoted by $C_B A$ such as

$$C_B A = \{x: Q(x) \wedge \sim P(x)\}$$

The shaded region in Figure 2.3 illustrates the complement of ***A*** **r**espect to ***B***.

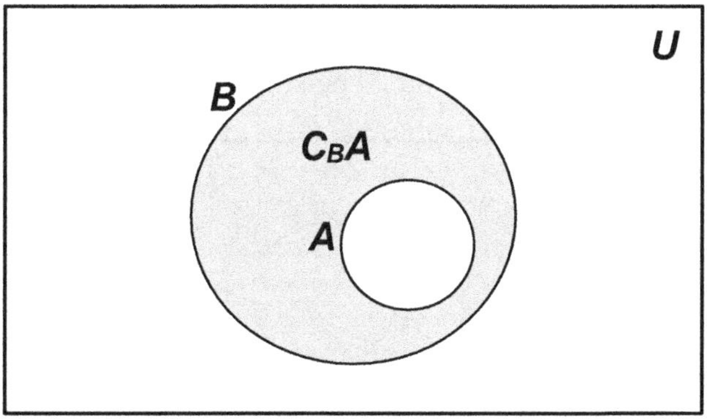

Figure 2.3

In most situations we need to define the complement of a set with respect to the universal set. We earlier stated that every set is a subset of the universal set. Therefore, for every set there exists a complement with respect to the universal set.

Thus, given the set A the complement of A respect to the universal set is usually denoted as A^c. However, sometimes we can also find notations such as $\bar{A}$ or A'. According to the definition and recalling that the universal set is usually denoted as U, in this case we have that

$$\mathbf{A}^c = \{x: x \in \mathbf{U} \wedge x \notin \mathbf{A}\}$$

When the set A is defined by comprehension, the formal definition is as follows:

Given the set A such that

$$\mathbf{A} = \{x: \; P(x)\}$$

and the universal set U such that $A \subseteq U$. The *complement of A respect to U* is the set denoted by A^c and such that

$$\mathbf{A}^c = \{x: \sim P(x)\}$$

Figure 2.4 illustrates this definition. The shaded area corresponds to A^c.

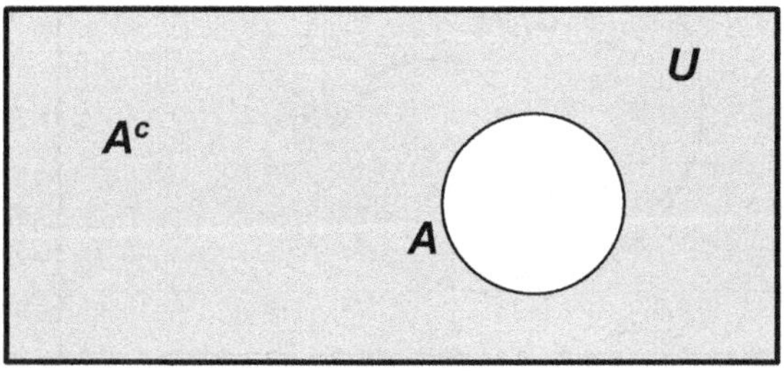

Figure 2.4

Examples

Given the sets:

$$\mathbf{A} = \{x: x \in \boldsymbol{N} \wedge x < 20\}$$

$$\mathbf{B} = \{x: x \in \boldsymbol{N} \wedge x \leq 50\}$$

We can verify that $\boldsymbol{A} \subseteq \boldsymbol{B}$. Therefore, there exists a complement of $\boldsymbol{A}$ respect to $\boldsymbol{B}$ denoted by $\mathbf{C}_{\boldsymbol{B}}\boldsymbol{A}$ such that

$$C_B A = \{x: x \in \boldsymbol{N} \wedge 20 \leq x \leq 50\}$$

By considering $\boldsymbol{A}$ and $\boldsymbol{B}$ given above and $\boldsymbol{N}$ the universal set, let us define their respective complements $\boldsymbol{A}^c$ and $\boldsymbol{B}^c$. These are

$$\mathbf{A}^c = \{x: x \in \boldsymbol{N} \wedge x \geq 20\}$$

$$\mathbf{B}^c = \{x: x \in \boldsymbol{N} \wedge x > 50\}$$

The complement of empty set

By recalling that the empty set can be defined by a contradiction such as

$$\varnothing = \{x: P(x) \wedge \sim P(x)\}$$

And that the universal set can be defined by a tautology, then, according to the definition of the complement set and the De Morgan law, we have that

$$\varnothing^C = \{x: \sim [P(x) \wedge \sim P(x)]\}$$

$$= \{x: [\sim P(x) \vee P(x)]\}$$

$$= \mathbf{U}$$

Thus, we can conclude that the complement of an empty set is the universal set.

The complement of the universal set

By applying the same procedure as before, we can prove that the complement of a universal set is an empty set. This is

$$\mathbf{U}^c = \varnothing$$

Properties of the complement of a subset

1) *Involution*

   Given any set $\boldsymbol{A}$, it is verified that

$$(\mathbf{A}^c)^c = \mathbf{A}$$

   Proof:

   Assuming that $\boldsymbol{A}$ is defined by $P(x)$, and according to the definition of complement and the double negation law, we have that

$$\begin{aligned}(\mathbf{A}^c)^c &= \{x\!: \sim [\sim P(x)]\} \\ &= \{x\!: P(x)\} \\ &= \mathbf{A}\end{aligned}$$

2) Assuming that the sets $\boldsymbol{A}$ and $\boldsymbol{B}$ are defined by $P(x)$ and $Q(x)$ respectively, it is verified that

$$\mathbf{A} \subseteq \mathbf{B} \Leftrightarrow \mathbf{B}^c \subseteq \mathbf{A}^c$$

   Proof:

   By recalling the definition of set inclusion, we know that

$$(\mathbf{A} \subseteq \mathbf{B}) \Leftrightarrow [P(x) \Rightarrow Q(x)]$$

   Then, we also know that

$$(\mathbf{B^c} \subseteq \mathbf{A^c}) \Leftrightarrow [\sim Q(x) \Rightarrow \sim P(x)]$$

According to the law of equivalence between the statement of an implication and its contrapositive form, it is verified that

$$\{[P(x) \Rightarrow Q(x)] \Leftrightarrow [\sim Q(x) \Rightarrow \sim P(x)]\}$$

Therefore

$$\mathbf{A} \subseteq \mathbf{B} \Leftrightarrow \mathbf{B^c} \subseteq \mathbf{A^c}$$

SET OF PARTS OF A SET

The *set of parts* of a given set ***A*** is the set of all possible subsets of ***A***. This set is denoted by ***P(A)*** and can be defined as follows:

$$\mathbf{P(A)} = \{\mathbf{X}: \mathbf{X} \subseteq A\}$$

X denotes a generic set.

According to the reflexive property of inclusion, every set is a subset of itself. Therefore, the following is true

$$\mathbf{A} \in \mathbf{P(A)}$$

Also, since the empty set is a subset of any other set, then

$$\varnothing \in \mathbf{P(A)}$$

Example

Let ***A*** be the following the set

$$\mathbf{A} = \{1, 2, 3\}$$

In this case ***P(A)*** is the following set:

$$\mathbf{P(A)} = \{\varnothing, \{1\}, \{2\}, \{3\}, \{1, 2\}, \{1, 3\}, \{2, 3\}, \mathbf{A}\}$$

Number of elements of the set of parts

To get a formula that allows us to know the total number of elements of the set of parts of a given set, we use combinatorial numbers.

Let us suppose that the given set ***A*** has n elements. There is only one subset with no element which is the empty set. This can be represented by

$$\binom{n}{0} = 1$$

There are n subsets with only one element. This is represented by

$$\binom{n}{1} = n$$

For subsets with two elements, we use

$$\binom{n}{2} = \frac{n!}{2!(n-2)!}$$

Similarly, for subsets with three elements we have

$$\binom{n}{3} = \frac{n!}{3!(n-3)!}$$

And so on until we get the number of subsets with n elements which is only the set ***A*** itself and that number is represented by

$$\binom{n}{n} = 1$$

Therefore, the total number of subsets of the set of parts is equal to the sum of all those numbers. This sum is

$$\binom{n}{0}+\binom{n}{1}+\binom{n}{2}+\binom{n}{3}+\ldots+\binom{n}{n}=\sum_{i=0}^{n}\binom{n}{i}=2^n$$

This result can be proved by using the binomial formula:

$$(x+y)^n = \sum_{i=0}^{n}\binom{n}{i}x^i y^{n-i}$$

So, by doing

$$2^n = (1+1)^n$$

and applying the binomial formula we get

$$(1+1)^n = \sum_{i=0}^{n}\binom{n}{i}1^i 1^{n-i} = \sum_{i=0}^{n}\binom{n}{i}$$

This proves the above result.

Example

In the previous example we have the set ***A*** such that

A = {1, 2, 3}

So, ***A*** has 3 elements. This is $n = 3$. Then, by applying the results we got earlier, the number of elements of ***P(A)*** is

$$2^3 = 8$$

Therefore, there are 8 possible subsets of ***A*** which form the set ***P(A)***.

EXERCISES II

1. Determine whether the following pairs of sets are equal or not:

a) $\mathbf{A} = \{x: x \in \boldsymbol{N} \wedge 5 \mid x \wedge x < 20\}$
$\mathbf{B} = \{10, 5, 15\}$

b) $\mathbf{C} = \{\text{even numbers}\}$
$\mathbf{D} = \{x: x \in \boldsymbol{N} \wedge 2 \mid x\}$

c) $\mathbf{E} = \{x: x \in \boldsymbol{N} \wedge x + 5 \leq 15\}$
$\mathbf{F} = \{x: x \in \boldsymbol{N} \wedge x < 10\}$

2. Determine whether the following equalities are true or false. Explain your answers.

a) $\{p\} = \{p, 0\}$ *b)* $\{p\} = \{p, \varnothing\}$ *c)* $\{\varnothing\} = \{\ \}$

d) $\{\ \} = \varnothing$ *e)* $\varnothing = \{\varnothing\}$ *f)* $\{x: x \in \boldsymbol{R} \wedge x^2 < 0\} = \varnothing$

3. Determine the inclusion relationships that are verified between the following sets:

$\mathbf{A} = \{1, 2, a, f\}$ $\mathbf{B} = \{2, f\}$ $\mathbf{C} = \{1, f, 3\}$ $\mathbf{D} = \{1, f\}$

4. Given the following diagrams, properly place within them each element according to the information given on the right side.

a)

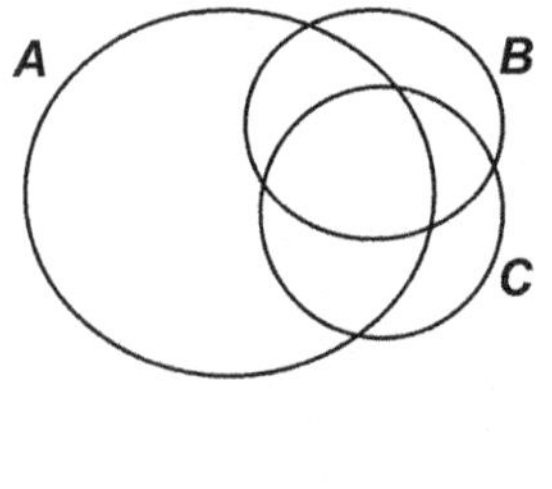

$a \in A,\ a \in B,\ a \notin C$
$b \notin A,\ b \notin B,\ b \in C$
$c \in A,\ c \in B,\ c \in C$
$d \notin A,\ d \in B,\ d \in C$
$e \in A,\ e \notin B,\ e \in C$

a)

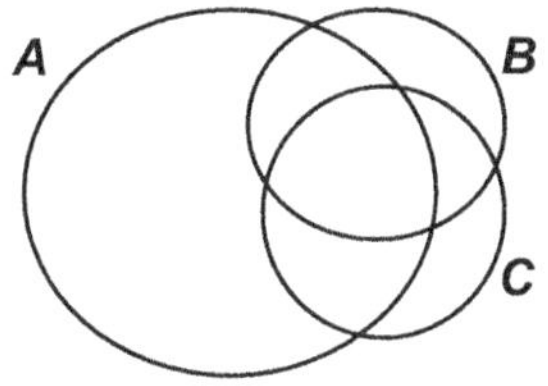

$a \in A$, $a \in B$, $a \in C$
$b \notin A$, $b \in B$, $b \in C$
$c \in A$, $c \notin B$, $c \in C$
$d \notin A$, $d \notin B$, $d \in C$
$e \in A$, $e \notin B$, $e \notin C$
$f \in A$, $f \in B$, $f \notin C$

b)

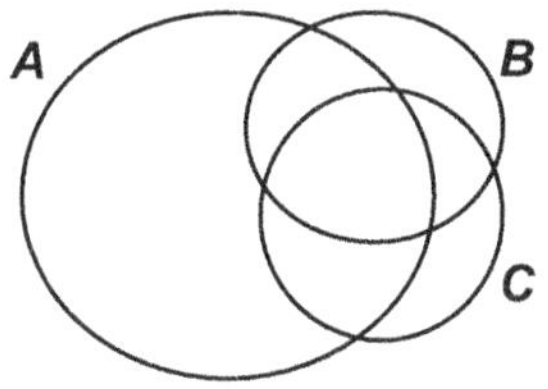

$a \in A$, $a \notin B$, $a \notin C$
$b \in A$, $b \in B$, $b \notin C$
$c \in A$, $c \in B$, $c \in C$
$d \notin A$, $d \in B$, $d \in C$
$e \in A$, $e \notin B$, $e \in C$
$f \notin A$, $f \in B$, $f \notin C$

5. Determine the inclusion relationships that are verified between the following sets:

   F: The set of four-digits numbers with at least two of the digits equal to zero.
   G: The set of four-digits numbers with at least one of the digits equal to zero.
   H: The set of four-digit numbers with two of the digits equal to zero and the others different from zero.

6. Given the following set:

$$\mathbf{A} = \{a, b, c\}$$

   Determine whether the following propositions are true or false. Explain.

$a \in \mathbf{A}$	$c \subset \mathbf{A}$	$\{b\} \in \mathbf{A}$
$\{b\} \subset \mathbf{A}$	$\{a, b, c\} \notin \mathbf{A}$	$\{a, b, c\} \subseteq \mathbf{A}$

7. Let **A** *and* **B** be any two sets. Write the definition for

$$\mathbf{A} \not\subseteq \mathbf{B} \text{ } (\mathbf{A} \text{ is not a subset of } \mathbf{B})$$

8. Given the following sets:

$\mathbf{A} = \{r, s, t, u, v, w\}$ $\mathbf{B} = \{u, v, w, x, y, z\}$

$\mathbf{C} = \{s, u, y, z\}$ $\mathbf{D} = \{u, v\}$

$\mathbf{E} = \{s, u\}$ $\mathbf{F} = \{s\}$

Let **X** be an unknown set.

Determine which of the sets given above is equal to **X** based on the information provided in each of the following cases:

a) $\mathbf{X} \subset \mathbf{A} \wedge \mathbf{X} \subset \mathbf{B}$

b) $\mathbf{X} \not\subset \mathbf{B} \wedge \mathbf{X} \subset \mathbf{C}$

c) $\mathbf{X} \not\subset A \wedge \mathbf{X} \not\subset \mathbf{C}$

d) $\mathbf{X} \subset B \wedge \mathbf{X} \not\subset \mathbf{C}$

9. Is it true or false that every set contains at least two subsets? Why?

10. Given the set

$$K = \{500, 934, 1000\}$$

Determine all possible sets L such that

$$\{500\} \subset L \wedge L \subset K \wedge \mathrm{L} \neq K$$

11. Assume that the universal set is constituted by the letters that form the word "*administración*"[1]. Determine the complement of each of the following sets:

---

[1] This word is the Spanish translation of the word "Administration" in English.

a) $\mathbf{A} = \{o, m, i, t, a, s\}$ $\mathbf{B} = \{m, i, n, i, s, t, r, o\}$

$\mathbf{C} = \{n, o, c, t, r, a, s, m, i, d\}$

b) The empty set

c) $\{1, 3, z\}$

12. Determine the set of parts of each of the following sets:

$\mathbf{A} = \{a, 3, p\}$ $\mathbf{B} = \{5, x\}$

$\mathbf{C} = \{x: x \in N \wedge x \text{ is odd} \wedge x < 3\}$

$\mathbf{D} = \{x: x \in N \wedge 5 \leq x \leq 8\}$

13. Given the set:

$$\mathbf{B} = \{\text{EARTH, WIND, FIRE}\}$$

Determine the set of parts of *B*. Explain why the following propositions are true:

a) $\varnothing \in \mathbf{P(B)} \wedge \varnothing \notin \mathbf{B}$

b) $\{\mathbf{B}\} \notin \mathbf{B} \wedge \{\mathbf{B}\} \not\subset \mathbf{B} \wedge \mathbf{B} \in \mathbf{P(B)}$

c) **B** is an element not a subset of **P(B)**

d) $\{\text{EARTH}\} \notin \mathbf{B} \wedge \{\text{EARTH}\} \in \mathbf{P(B)}$

14. Let *A*, *B* and *C* be any three sets. Determine the truth value of each of the following statements. Prove the statements that are true and provide a counterexample for those which are false.

a) If $x \in \mathbf{A}$ and $\mathbf{B} \subset \mathbf{A}$ and $\mathbf{B} \subset \mathbf{C}$, then $x \in \mathbf{C}$

b) If $\mathbf{A} \subset \mathbf{B}$ and $\mathbf{B} \subset \mathbf{C}$, then $\mathbf{A} \subset \mathbf{C}$

c) If $\mathbf{A} \subset \mathbf{B}$ and $\mathbf{A} \subset \mathbf{C}$, then $\mathbf{A} = \mathbf{C}$

d) If $x \in \mathbf{C}$ and $\mathbf{C} \subset \mathbf{A}$, then $x \in \mathbf{A}$.

e) If $x \in \mathbf{A}$ and $\mathbf{A} \subset \mathbf{B}$ and $x \in \mathbf{C}$, then $\mathbf{C} \subset \mathbf{B}$.

SET OPERATIONS

Set operations are combinations of given sets to produce new ones. There are four basic operations: Intersection, Union, Difference, and Symmetric Difference.

Intersection

Given two sets ***A*** and ***B***, the *intersection of* ***A*** *and* ***B*** is a new set formed by all elements that belong to both ***A*** and ***B*** and no other elements. In other words, the intersection of ***A*** and ***B*** is the set formed only by all elements that sets ***A*** and ***B*** have in common.

The symbol used to represent the intersection of sets looks like an upside-down U.

According to the definition, the intersection of ***A*** and ***B*** is the set

$$\mathbf{A} \cap \mathbf{B} = \{x: x \in \mathbf{A} \wedge x \in \mathbf{B}\}$$

Therefore, this definition establishes that

$$x \in \mathbf{A} \cap \mathbf{B} \Leftrightarrow (x \in \mathbf{A} \wedge x \in \mathbf{B})$$

Being ***A*** and ***B*** defined by the rules *P(x)* and *Q(x)* respectively, we can also write that

$$x \in \mathbf{A} \cap \mathbf{B} \Leftrightarrow [P(x) \wedge Q(x)]$$

In this case, an element x belongs to the intersection of ***A*** and ***B***, if and only if, it makes the conjunction of *P(x)* and *Q(x)* true.

By applying the truth table that defines the conjunction of two propositions that we presented earlier in Chapter 1, the intersection of sets ***A*** and ***B*** can also be defined by the following table:

P(x) **(A)**	***Q(x)*** **(B)**	***P(x) ∧ Q(x)*** **(A∩B)**
T	**T**	T
T	**F**	F
F	**T**	F
F	**F**	F

We can observe that the intersection of *A* and *B* corresponds to the first row of the table which determines the shaded region in the Venn diagram shown in Figure 2.5 below.

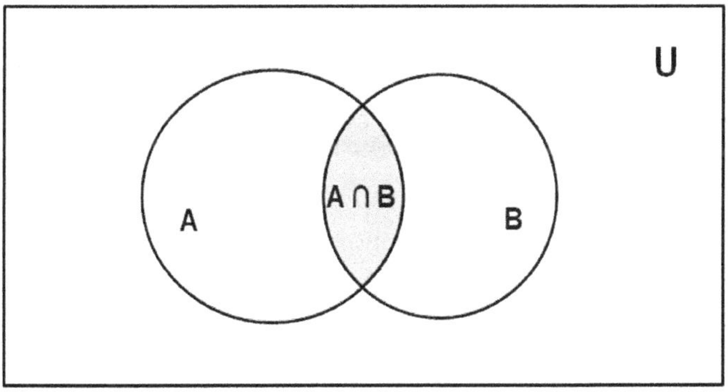

Figure 2.5

The formal definition for the intersection of two sets is as follows:

Given the sets *A* and *B* such that

$$A = \{x: P(x)\} \qquad B = \{x: Q(x)\}$$

$$A \cap B = \{x: P(x) \wedge Q(x)\}$$

Example

Let ***A*** and ***B*** be the sets such that

$$\mathbf{A} = \{x : x \in \boldsymbol{Z} \wedge x \geq -5\}$$

$$\mathbf{B} = \{x : x \in \boldsymbol{Z} \wedge x < 4\}$$

The intersection of ***A*** and ***B*** is the set $A \cap B$ such that

$$\mathbf{A} \cap \mathbf{B} = \{x : x \in \boldsymbol{Z} \wedge -5 \leq x < 4\}$$

According to the simplification law studied in Chapter 1, we know that

$$P(x) \wedge Q(x) \Rightarrow P(x)$$

and

$$P(x) \wedge Q(x) \Rightarrow Q(x)$$

Therefore, based on this law of logic and the respective definitions of inclusion and intersection, we conclude that

$$(\mathbf{A} \cap \mathbf{B}) \subseteq \mathbf{A} \quad \text{and} \quad (\mathbf{A} \cap \mathbf{B}) \subseteq \mathbf{B}$$

This is, in words, that the intersection of two any sets is a subset of each of them. These relationships are always true regardless of any condition.

Disjoint sets

Given the sets ***A*** and ***B***, we say that they are *disjoint*, if and only if, they have no common elements. Therefore, the intersection of disjoint sets is the empty set. Thus, we state that

A and B are *disjoint* sets $\Leftrightarrow$ A∩B = ∅

Example

Given the following sets:

$$\mathbf{A} = \{x: x \in \boldsymbol{Z} \wedge x \geq 5\}$$

$$\mathbf{B} = \{x: x \in \boldsymbol{Z} \wedge x < 4\}$$

Since there are no common elements between ***A*** and ***B***, we can state that **A∩B** = ∅ which means that *A* and *B* are disjoint sets.

Properties of intersection of sets

Given the sets ***A***, ***B*** and ***C*** such that

$$\mathbf{A} = \{x: P(x)\} \qquad \mathbf{B} = \{x: Q(x)\} \qquad \mathbf{C} = \{x: R(x)\}$$

The following properties are satisfied:

1. *Idempotent*

   Every set ***A*** satisfies that

   $$\mathbf{A \cap A = A}$$

   This property is supported by the idempotent law of logic. This is

   $$P(x) \wedge P(x) \equiv P(x)$$

2. *Commutative*

   $$\mathbf{A \cap B = B \cap A}$$

   The commutative law of conjunction supports this property. This law is

   $$P(x) \wedge Q(x) \equiv Q(x) \wedge P(x)$$

3. *Associative*

$$\mathbf{A} \cap (\mathbf{B} \cap \mathbf{C}) = (\mathbf{A} \cap \mathbf{B}) \cap \mathbf{C}$$

Supported by the associative law of logic

$$P(x) \wedge [Q(x) \wedge R(x)] \equiv [P(x) \wedge Q(x)] \wedge R(x)$$

4. $(A \subseteq B) \Leftrightarrow [(A \cap B) = A]$

Proof:

Let us prove first that

$$(\mathbf{A} \subseteq \mathbf{B}) \Rightarrow [(\mathbf{A} \cap \mathbf{B}) = \mathbf{A}]$$

By applying the antisymmetric property of inclusion to the consequent, the above implication can be rewritten as

$$(\mathbf{A} \subseteq \mathbf{B}) \Rightarrow \{[(\mathbf{A} \cap \mathbf{B}) \subseteq \mathbf{A}] \wedge [\mathbf{A} \subseteq (\mathbf{A} \cap \mathbf{B})]\}$$

Since it was shown earlier that

$$(\mathbf{A} \cap \mathbf{B}) \subseteq \mathbf{A}$$

We only need to prove now that

$$(\mathbf{A} \subseteq \mathbf{B}) \Rightarrow [\mathbf{A} \subseteq (\mathbf{A} \cap \mathbf{B})]$$

Let us proceed as follows:

$\mathbf{A} \subseteq \mathbf{B}$		
$(\mathbf{A} \subseteq \mathbf{B})$	$\Rightarrow [P(x) \Rightarrow Q(x)]$	By definition of inclusion
$[P(x) \Rightarrow Q(x)]$	$\Rightarrow \{P(x) \Rightarrow [P(x) \wedge Q(x)]\}$	(Logical equivalence)
$\{P(x) \Rightarrow [P(x) \wedge Q(x)]\}$	$\Rightarrow [\mathbf{A} \subseteq (\mathbf{A} \cap \mathbf{B})]$	By def of both incl and intersect
$\therefore \mathbf{A} \subseteq (\mathbf{A} \cap \mathbf{B})$		

The logical equivalence $(P \to Q) \equiv [P \to (P \wedge Q)]$ can be proven by building the corresponding truth table.

Let us now prove the converse form. This is:

$$[(\mathbf{A} \cap \mathbf{B}) = \mathbf{A}] \Rightarrow (\mathbf{A} \subseteq \mathbf{B})$$

Then

$(\mathbf{A} \cap B) = \mathbf{A}$		
$[(\mathbf{A} \cap \mathbf{B}) = \mathbf{A}]$	$\Rightarrow [\mathbf{A} = (\mathbf{A} \cap \mathbf{B})]$	By commutativity of equality
$[\mathbf{A} = (\mathbf{A} \cap \mathbf{B})]$	$\Rightarrow [\mathbf{A} \subseteq (\mathbf{A} \cap \mathbf{B})]$	By reflexive prop of inclusion
$[\mathbf{A} \subseteq (\mathbf{A} \cap \mathbf{B})]$	$\Rightarrow \{P(x) \Rightarrow [P(x) \wedge Q(x)]\}$	By def. of both incl. and inter
$\{P(x) \Rightarrow [P(x) \wedge Q(x)]\}$	$\Rightarrow [P(x) \Rightarrow Q(x)]$	By simplification law of conjunc
$[P(x) \Rightarrow Q(x)]$	$\Rightarrow (\mathbf{A} \subseteq \mathbf{B})$	By definition of inclusion
$\therefore \mathbf{A} \subseteq \mathbf{B}$		

This completes the demonstration.

5. *Identity (neutral) element for intersection of sets*

In general, we can say that set operations are operations performed between elements of the set of parts of the universal set U that we have denoted by ***P(U)***. In other words, they are operations performed between subsets of U.

In the case of intersection of sets, the *identity or neutral element* is the element of ***P(U)*** whose intersection with any other element ***A*** of ***P(U)*** reproduces the same element ***A***. This element for intersection is the universal set ***U***. Therefore, it is satisfied that

$$\mathbf{A} \cap \mathbf{U} = \mathbf{U} \cap \mathbf{A} = \mathbf{A}$$

This is a corollary of *property 4*. In fact, we have already said that

$$\mathbf{A} \subseteq \mathbf{U}$$

Therefore, according to *property 4* we have that

$$(\mathbf{A} \subseteq \mathbf{U}) \Leftrightarrow [(\mathbf{A} \cap \mathbf{U}) = \mathbf{A}]$$

This result, along with the commutative property of intersection of sets, proves that *the universal set is the identity or neutral element of intersection of sets.*

Two additional characteristics of the empty set

Based on the definition of intersection of sets, we can now list two additional characteristics of the empty set. These are:

1. For any set A, it is always verified that

$$\mathbf{A} \cap \varnothing = \varnothing$$

Proof:

We have already seen that

$$\varnothing \subseteq \mathbf{A}$$

Therefore, according to *property 4* we have that

$$(\varnothing \subseteq \mathbf{A}) \Leftrightarrow [(\mathbf{A} \cap \varnothing) = \varnothing]$$

This proves the statement.

2. For any set A it is verified that

$$\mathbf{A} \cap \mathbf{A}^c = \varnothing$$

Since A^c is defined as the set formed by all those elements that belong to the universal set that are not members of A, this means that A and A^c are disjoint sets and consequently the result of their intersection is the empty set.

Union

Given two any sets A and B, the *union of A and B* is a new set formed by all elements that belong to either A or B or to both.

The symbol used to represent the union of sets looks like an U. Thus, according to this definition, the union of A and B is the set such that

$$\mathbf{A} \cup \mathbf{B} = \{x: x \in \mathbf{A} \vee x \in \mathbf{B}\}$$

Therefore, an element belongs to the union of two sets, if and only if, it belongs to at least one of them. This means that the union is the set formed by all elements of both sets taken altogether. This definition establishes that

$$x \in \mathbf{A} \cup \mathbf{B} \Leftrightarrow (x \in \mathbf{A} \vee x \in \mathbf{B})$$

When A and B are defined by the rules $P(x)$ and $Q(x)$ respectively, we can also write that

$$x \in \mathbf{A} \cup \mathbf{B} \Leftrightarrow [P(x) \vee Q(x)]$$

This means that an element x belongs to the union of A and B, if and only if, it makes the inclusive disjunction of $P(x)$ and $Q(x)$ true.

By applying the truth table that defines the inclusive disjunction of two propositions that we presented earlier in Chapter 1, the union of sets A and B can also be defined by the following table:

$P(x)$ (A)	$Q(x)$ (B)	$P(x) \vee Q(x)$ (AUB)
T	T	T
T	F	T
F	T	T
F	F	F

We can observe that the union of ***A*** and ***B*** corresponds to the first three rows of the table which determine the three shaded regions in the Venn diagram shown in Figure 2.6.

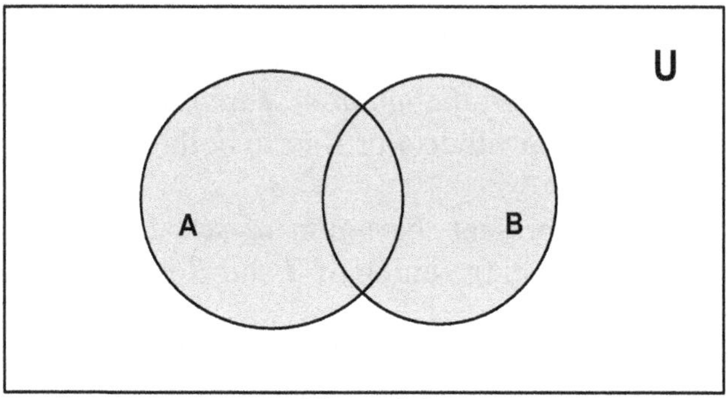

Figure 2.6

If ***A*** and ***B*** were disjoint sets, the combination shown in the first row of the previous truth table is not possible. In this case, only two shaded regions are determined in the Venn diagram. Figure 2.7 shows an example of union of disjoint sets.

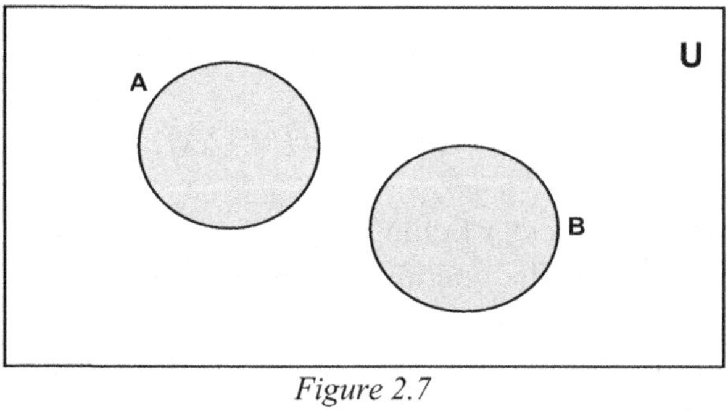

Figure 2.7

The formal definition for the union of two sets is as follows:

Given the sets *A* and *B* such that

$$A = \{x: P(x)\} \quad \text{and} \quad B = \{x: Q(x)\}$$

$$A \cup B = \{x: P(x) \vee Q(x)\}$$

Example

Let us have the following sets:

$$\mathbf{A} = \{x: x \in \boldsymbol{Z} \wedge x \leq -2\}$$

$$\mathbf{B} = \{x: x \in \boldsymbol{Z} \wedge x > 2\}$$

The union of ***A*** and ***B*** is the set

$$\mathbf{A \cup B} = \{x: x \in \boldsymbol{Z} \wedge (x \leq -2 \vee x > 2)\}$$

The union of two sets includes both sets and their intersection

This is

$$A \subseteq (A \cup B) \qquad B \subseteq (A \cup B) \qquad (A \cap B) \subseteq (A \cup B)$$

The definitions of inclusion, intersection, and union, along with the following laws of logic:

$$P(x) \Rightarrow [P(x) \vee Q(x)] \qquad \text{(Addition)}$$

$$Q(x) \Rightarrow [P(x) \vee Q(x)] \qquad \text{(Addition)}$$

$$[P(x) \wedge Q(x)] \Rightarrow [P(x) \vee Q(x)] \quad \text{(Simplification and addition)}$$

support the results presented above. They are true for any ***A*** and ***B*** regardless of any condition.

Properties of union of sets

Given the sets A, B and C defined as

$$A = \{x: P(x)\} \qquad B = \{x: Q(x)\} \qquad C = \{x: R(x)\}$$

The following properties are satisfied:

1. *Idempotent*

   Every set A satisfies the following:

   $$\mathbf{A \cup A = A}$$

   This property is supported by the idempotent law of logic:

   $$P(x) \vee P(x) \equiv P(x)$$

2. *Commutative*

   $$\mathbf{A \cup B = B \cup A}$$

   Supported by the commutative law of disjunction:

   $$P(x) \vee Q(x) \equiv Q(x) \vee P(x)$$

3. *Associative*

   $$A \cup (B \cup C) = (A \cup B) \cup C$$

   Supported by the associative law of logic:

   $$P(x) \vee [Q(x) \vee R(x)] \equiv [P(x) \vee Q(x)] \vee R(x)$$

4. $(\mathbf{A} \subseteq \mathbf{B}) \Leftrightarrow [(\mathbf{A} \cup \mathbf{B}) = \mathbf{B}]$

Proof:

Let us prove first the following:

$$(\mathbf{A} \subseteq \mathbf{B}) \Rightarrow [(\mathbf{A} \cup \mathbf{B}) = \mathbf{B}]$$

By applying the antisymmetric property of inclusion to the consequent of the above implication, it can be rewritten as

$$(\mathbf{A} \subseteq \mathbf{B}) \Rightarrow \{[(\mathbf{A} \cup \mathbf{B}) \subseteq \mathbf{B}] \wedge [\mathbf{B} \subseteq (\mathbf{A} \cup \mathbf{B})]\}$$

We earlier saw that for any A and B it is always true that

$$\mathbf{B} \subseteq (\mathbf{A} \cup \mathbf{B})$$

Therefore, we only need to prove that

$$(\mathbf{A} \subseteq \mathbf{B}) \Rightarrow [(\mathbf{A} \cup \mathbf{B}) \subseteq \mathbf{B}]$$

Let us proceed as follows:

$\mathbf{A} \subseteq \mathbf{B}$		
$(\mathbf{A} \subseteq \mathbf{B})$	$\Rightarrow [P(x) \Rightarrow Q(x)]$	By definition of inclusion
$[P(x) \Rightarrow Q(x)]$	$\Rightarrow \{[P(x) \vee Q(x)] \Rightarrow Q(x)\}$	(Logical equivalence)
$\{[P(x) \vee Q(x)] \Rightarrow Q(x)\}$	$\Rightarrow [(\mathbf{A} \cup \mathbf{B}) \subseteq \mathbf{B}]$	By def. of both union and incl

$\therefore\ (\mathbf{A} \cup \mathbf{B}) \subseteq \mathbf{B}$

The logical equivalence $(P \rightarrow Q) \equiv [(P \vee Q) \rightarrow \mathrm{Q}]$ can be proven by building the corresponding truth table.

Let us now prove the converse form:

$$[(\mathbf{A} \cup \mathbf{B}) = \mathbf{B}] \Rightarrow (\mathbf{A} \subseteq \mathbf{B})$$

This is

$(\mathbf{A} \cup \mathbf{B}) = \mathbf{B}$

$[(\mathbf{A} \cup B) = \mathbf{B}]$	$\Rightarrow [(\mathbf{A} \cup \mathbf{B}) \subseteq \mathbf{B}]$	By reflexive prop of inclusion
$[(\mathbf{A} \cup B) \subseteq \mathbf{B}]$	$\Rightarrow \{[P(x) \vee Q(x)] \Rightarrow Q(x)\}$	By def of both union and incl
$\{[P(x) \vee Q(x)] \Rightarrow Q(x)\}$	$\Rightarrow [P(x) \Rightarrow Q(x)]$	(Logical equivalence)
$[P(x) \Rightarrow Q(x)]$	$\Rightarrow (\mathbf{A} \subseteq \mathbf{B})$	By definition of inclusion

$\therefore \mathbf{A} \subseteq \mathbf{B}$

The logical equivalence $[(p \vee q) \rightarrow q] \equiv (p \rightarrow q)$ can be proven by building the corresponding truth table.

This completes the demonstration.

5. *Identity (neutral) element for union of sets*

In the case of union of sets, the *identity or neutral element* is the element of ***P(U)*** whose union with any other element ***A*** of ***P(U)*** reproduces the same element ***A***. This element for union is the empty set $\varnothing$. Therefore, it is satisfied that

$$\mathbf{A} \cup \varnothing = \varnothing \cup \mathbf{A} = \mathbf{A}$$

This property is a corollary of *property 4*. By recalling that the empty set is a subset of any other set, it can be verified according to *property 4* that

$$(\varnothing \subseteq \mathbf{A}) \Leftrightarrow [(\mathbf{A} \cup \varnothing) = \mathbf{A}]$$

Thus, along with the commutative property of union of sets, it is proven that $\varnothing$ is the neutral element for union of sets.

6. Given any set A it is verified that

$$\mathbf{A} \cup \mathbf{A}^c = \mathbf{U}$$

Proof:

To prove this equality, we must apply the antisymmetric property of inclusion.

$$[(\mathbf{A} \cup \mathbf{A}^c) = \mathbf{U}] \Leftrightarrow \{[(\mathbf{A} \cup \mathbf{A}^c) \subseteq \mathbf{U})] \wedge [\mathbf{U} \subseteq (\mathbf{A} \cup \mathbf{A}^c)]\}$$

Let us assume that A is defined by comprehension such that

$$\mathbf{A} = \{x\text{: } P(x)\}$$

Therefore

$$\mathbf{A}^c = \{x\text{: } \sim P(x)\} \quad \text{and} \quad \mathbf{U} = \{x\text{: } P(x) \vee \sim P(x)\}$$

Then

$$\begin{array}{ll} x \in (\mathbf{A} \cup \mathbf{A}^c) & \\ x \in (\mathbf{A} \cup \mathbf{A}^c) & \Rightarrow [P(x) \vee \sim P(x)] \\ [P(x) \vee \sim P(x)] & \Rightarrow x \in \mathbf{U} \\ \hline \therefore x \in \mathbf{U} & \end{array}$$

This proves that

$$[x \in (\mathbf{A} \cup \mathbf{A}^c) \Rightarrow x \in \mathbf{U}] \equiv [(\mathbf{A} \cup \mathbf{A}^c) \subseteq \mathbf{U}]$$

The converse form is

$$\begin{array}{ll} x \in \mathbf{U} & \\ x \in \mathbf{U} & \Rightarrow [P(x) \vee \sim P(x)] \\ [P(x) \vee \sim P(x)] & \Rightarrow x \in (\mathbf{A} \cup \mathbf{A}^c) \\ \hline \therefore x \in (\mathbf{A} \cup \mathbf{A}^c) & \end{array}$$

This proves that

$$[x \in \mathbf{U} \Rightarrow x \in (\mathbf{A} \cup \mathbf{A}^c)] \equiv [(\mathbf{U} \subseteq (\mathbf{A} \cup \mathbf{A}^c)]$$

This completes the demonstration.

Properties that relate intersection, union, and complement

Given the sets **A**, **B** and **C** such that

$\mathbf{A} = \{x: P(x)\}$ $\quad\quad$ $\mathbf{B} = \{x: Q(x)\}$ $\quad\quad$ $\mathbf{C} = \{x: R(x)\}$

1. *Distributive*

   Intersection with respect to union

$$\mathbf{A} \cap (\mathbf{B} \cup \mathbf{C}) = (\mathbf{A} \cap \mathbf{B}) \cup (\mathbf{A} \cap \mathbf{C})$$

   Supported by the logical equivalence:

$$\{P(x) \wedge [Q(x) \vee R(x)]\} \equiv \{[P(x) \wedge Q(x)] \vee [P(x) \wedge R(x)]\}$$

   Union with respect to intersection

$$\mathbf{A} \cup (\mathbf{B} \cap \mathbf{C}) = (\mathbf{A} \cup \mathbf{B}) \cap (\mathbf{A} \cup \mathbf{C})$$

   Supported by the logical equivalence:

$$\{P(x) \vee [Q(x) \wedge R(x)]\} \equiv \{[P(x) \vee Q(x)] \wedge [P(x) \vee R(x)]\}$$

2. *De Morgan*

   a) $(\mathbf{A} \cap \mathbf{B})^c = \mathbf{A}^c \cup \mathbf{B}^c$

   Supported by the logical equivalence:

$$\sim [P(x) \wedge Q(x)] \equiv [\sim P(x) \vee \sim Q(x)]$$

b) $(\mathbf{A} \cup \mathbf{B})^c = \mathbf{A}^c \cap \mathbf{B}^c$

Supported by the logical equivalence:

$$\sim [P(x) \vee Q(x)] \equiv [\sim P(x) \wedge \sim Q(x)]$$

Difference

Given the sets ***A*** and ***B***, the *difference of **A** and **B*** is the set of all elements in ***A*** that do not belong to ***B***. We will denote the difference of ***A*** and ***B*** as follows:

$$\mathbf{A - B}$$

The above is the most frequent notation for the difference of sets found in the literature on Set Theory. However, sometimes it is found also denoted as ***A*** \ ***B***. According to the definition, we have that

$$x \in (\mathbf{A} - \mathbf{B}) \Leftrightarrow x \in \mathbf{A} \wedge x \notin \mathbf{B}$$

When ***A*** and ***B*** are defined by comprehension such that

$$\mathbf{A} = \{x: P(x)\} \text{ and } \quad \mathbf{B} = \{x: Q(x)\}$$

We can write the above statement as follows:

$$x \in (\mathbf{A} - \mathbf{B}) \Leftrightarrow P(x) \wedge \sim Q(x)$$

This means that an element belongs to the difference of ***A*** and ***B***, if and only if, it makes *P(x)* true and *Q(x)* false. In other words, the elements that constitute the difference of ***A*** and ***B*** are those that make the conjunction of *P(x)* and *~Q(x)* true.

By applying the truth table that defines the conjunction of two propositions that we presented earlier in Chapter 1, the difference of sets ***A*** and ***B*** can also be defined by the following table:

$P(x)$ (A)	$Q(x)$ (B)	$\sim Q(x)$ (B^c)	$P(x) \wedge \sim Q(x)$ (A – B)
T	T	F	F
T	F	T	T
F	T	F	F
F	F	T	F

We can see that the difference of ***A*** and ***B*** corresponds with the second row of the table which in turn determines the shaded region of the Venn diagram shown in Figure 2.8 below.

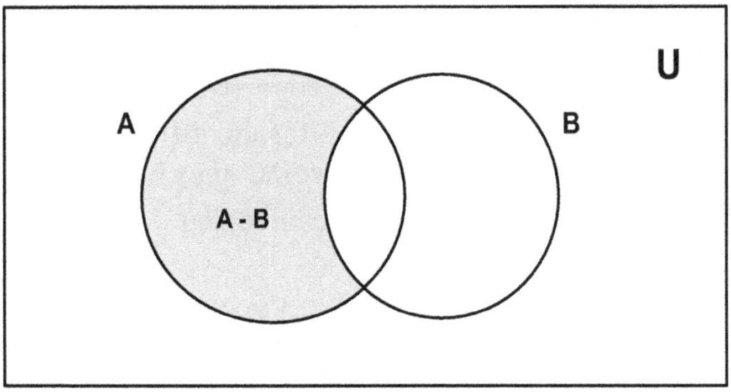

Figure 2.8

Thus, the formal definition for the difference of two sets can be stated as follows:

Given *A* and *B* such that

$$A = \{x: P(x)\} \qquad B = \{x: Q(x)\}$$

$$A - B = \{x: P(x) \wedge \sim Q(x)\}$$

The definition makes clear that the difference of sets does not satisfy commutativity. This is:

$$\mathbf{A - B \neq B - A}$$

This can be easily proven just by verifying that

$$[P(x) \wedge \sim Q(x)] \not\equiv [Q(x) \wedge \sim P(x)]$$

By using the truth table as we have done before, we have that

$P(x)$ (A)	$Q(x)$ (B)	$\sim P(x)$ $(A)^c$	$\sim P(x) \wedge Q(x)$ (B - A)
T	T	F	F
T	F	F	F
F	T	T	T
F	F	T	F

The difference ***B*** – ***A*** is illustrated in Figure 2.9. By comparing with Figure 2.8, we can verify that the difference of two sets is not commutative.

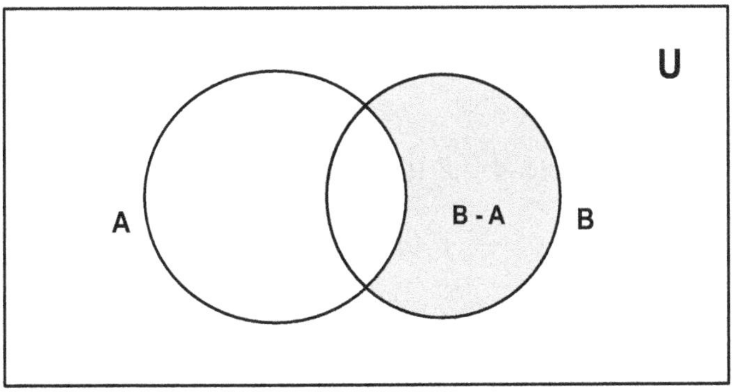

Figure 2.9

Example

Let ***A*** and ***B*** be the following sets:

$$\mathbf{A} = \{x\text{: } x \in \boldsymbol{Z} \wedge 0 < x \leq 9\}$$

$$\mathbf{B} = \{x\text{: } x \in \boldsymbol{Z} \wedge -4 \leq x \leq 4\}$$

The difference $\boldsymbol{A} - \boldsymbol{B}$ is

$$\mathbf{A} - \mathbf{B} = \{x\text{: } x \in \boldsymbol{Z} \wedge 5 \leq x \leq 9\} = \{5, 6, 7, 8, 9\}$$

While the difference $\boldsymbol{B} - \boldsymbol{A}$ is

$$\mathbf{B} - \mathbf{A} = \{x\text{: } x \in \boldsymbol{Z} \wedge -4 \leq x \leq 0\} = \{-4, -3, -2, -1, 0\}$$

Property

Given $\boldsymbol{A}$ and $\boldsymbol{B}$ such that

$$\mathbf{A} = \{x\text{: } P(x)\} \quad \text{and} \qquad \mathbf{B} = \{x\text{: } Q(x)\}$$

It is verified that

$$\mathbf{A} - \mathbf{B} = \mathbf{A} \cap \mathbf{B}^c$$

Proof:

In propositional language $\boldsymbol{A} - \boldsymbol{B}$ is defined as

$$P(x) \wedge \sim Q(x)$$

Since $\sim Q(x)$ defines $\boldsymbol{B}^c$, the conjunction above proves the property.

Likewise, it is verified that

$$\mathbf{B} - \mathbf{A} = \mathbf{B} \cap \mathbf{A}^c$$

Also, notice that if $\boldsymbol{A}$ and $\boldsymbol{B}$ are disjoint sets, then

$$\mathbf{A - B = A} \qquad \text{and} \qquad \mathbf{B - A = B}$$

Symmetric Difference

The *symmetric difference* of two sets ***A*** and ***B*** is a new set defined as the set of elements that belong to either ***A*** or ***B*** but not to both. It is usually denoted by ***A* Δ *B***. Therefore

$$x \in (\mathbf{A} \,\Delta\, \mathbf{B}) \Leftrightarrow x \in \mathbf{A} \veebar x \in \mathbf{B}$$

When ***A*** and ***B*** are defined by comprehension such that

$$\mathbf{A} = \{x\text{: } P(x)\} \quad \text{and} \qquad \mathbf{B} = \{x\text{: } Q(x)\}$$

We can write the above definition as follows:

$$x \in (\mathbf{A} \,\Delta\, \mathbf{B}) \Leftrightarrow P(x) \veebar Q(x)$$

This means that an element belongs to the symmetric difference of ***A*** and ***B***, if and only if, it makes true either *P(x*) or *Q(x)* but not both simultaneously. In other words, the elements that constitute the symmetric difference of ***A*** and ***B*** are those that make the exclusive disjunction of *P(x)* and *Q(x)* true.

By applying the truth table that defines the exclusive disjunction of two propositions that we presented earlier in Chapter 1, the symmetric difference of sets ***A*** and ***B*** can also be defined by the following table:

P(x) **(A)**	***Q(x)*** **B(x)**	***P(x)*** $\veebar$ ***Q(x)*** **(AΔB)**
T	**T**	F
T	**F**	T
F	**T**	T
F	**F**	F

We can see that the symmetric difference of ***A*** and ***B*** corresponds with both the second and third row of the table which in turn determine the shaded region of the Venn diagram shown in Figure 2.10 below.

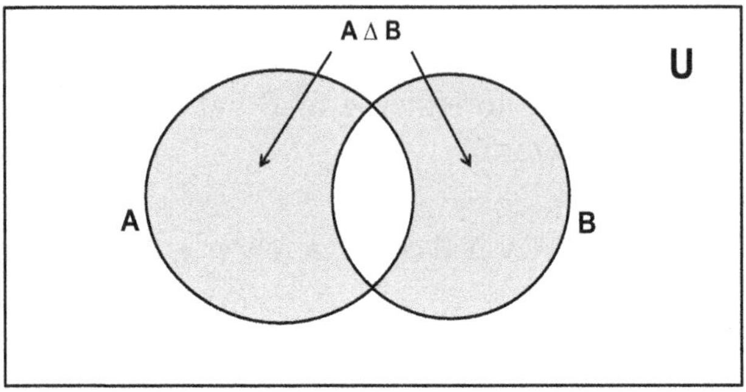

Figure 2.10

The formal definition for the symmetric difference of sets can be stated as follows:

Given *A* and *B* such that

$$A = \{x: P(x)\} \qquad B = \{x: Q(x)\}$$

$$A \, \Delta \, B = \{x: P(x) \veebar Q(x)\}$$

The symmetric difference can be written in different ways. According to the definition, an element belongs to the symmetric difference of sets ***A*** and ***B***, if and only if, it is in ***A*** but not in ***B*** or if it is in ***B*** but not in ***A***. By using symbols

$$x \in (\mathbf{A} \, \Delta \, \mathbf{B}) \Leftrightarrow (x \in \mathbf{A} \wedge x \notin \mathbf{B}) \vee (x \in \mathbf{B} \wedge x \notin \mathbf{A})$$

By applying the definition of the difference of sets, the above statement can also be written as

$$x \in (\mathbf{A} \, \Delta \, \mathbf{B}) \Leftrightarrow x \in (\mathbf{A} - \mathbf{B}) \vee x \in (\mathbf{B} - \mathbf{A})$$

Since the union of sets has been defined by an inclusive disjunction, the above statement can also be written as

$$x \in (\mathbf{A} \,\Delta\, \mathbf{B}) \Leftrightarrow x \in [(\mathbf{A} - \mathbf{B}) \cup (\mathbf{B} - \mathbf{A})]$$

Therefore, this means that

$$\text{A} \,\Delta\, \text{B} = (\text{A} - \text{B}) \cup (\text{B} - \text{A})$$

Likewise, it can be proven that

$$\text{A} \,\Delta\, \text{B} = (\text{A} \cap \text{B}^c) \cup (\text{B} \cap \text{A}^c)$$

$$\text{A} \,\Delta\, \text{B} = (\text{A} \cup \text{B}) - (\text{A} \cap \text{B})$$

Example

Let ***A*** and ***B*** be the same sets that we saw in the previous example:

$$\mathbf{A} = \{x \colon x \in \boldsymbol{Z} \wedge 0 < x \leq 9\}$$

$$\mathbf{B} = \{x \colon x \in \boldsymbol{Z} \wedge -4 \leq x \leq 4\}$$

The symmetric difference of ***A*** and ***B*** is the set:

$$\mathbf{A} \,\Delta\, \mathbf{B} = \{-4, -3, -2, -1, 0, 5, 6, 7, 8, 9\}$$

By using the results from the previous example, we confirm that in fact it is verified that

$$\mathbf{A} \,\Delta\, \mathbf{B} = \{5, 6, 7, 8, 9\} \cup \{-4, -3, -2, -1, 0\} = (\mathbf{A} - \mathbf{B}) \cup (\mathbf{B} - \mathbf{A})$$

Properties of symmetric difference

Let ***A***, ***B***, and ***C*** be the sets such that

$$\mathbf{A} = \{x\text{: } P(x)\} \qquad \mathbf{B} = \{x\text{: } Q(x)\} \qquad \mathbf{C} = \{x\text{: } R(x)\}$$

1. *Commutativity*

   It is verified that

$$\mathbf{A} \mathbin{\Delta} \mathbf{B} = \mathbf{B} \mathbin{\Delta} \mathbf{A}$$

   Supported by the commutative law of exclusive disjunction:

$$P(x) \veebar Q(x) \equiv Q(x) \veebar P(x)$$

2. *Associativity*

$$\mathbf{A} \mathbin{\Delta} (\mathbf{B} \mathbin{\Delta} \mathbf{C}) = (\mathbf{A} \mathbin{\Delta} \mathbf{B}) \mathbin{\Delta} \mathbf{C}$$

   Supported by the associative law of exclusive disjunction:

$$P(x) \veebar [Q(x) \veebar R(x)] \equiv [P(x) \veebar Q(x)] \veebar R(x)$$

3. *Identity (neutral) element for symmetric difference of sets*

   The empty set is neutral for the symmetric difference of sets since for any set A it is satisfied that

$$\mathbf{A} \mathbin{\Delta} \varnothing = \varnothing \mathbin{\Delta} \mathbf{A} = \mathbf{A}$$

   Proof:

$$\mathbf{A} \mathbin{\Delta} \varnothing = (\mathbf{A} \cap \varnothing^{c}) \cup (\varnothing \cap \mathbf{A}^{c})$$

$$= (\mathbf{A} \cap \mathbf{U}) \cup \varnothing$$

$$= \mathbf{A} \cap \mathbf{U}$$

$$= \mathbf{A}$$

4. *Inverse element for symmetric difference of sets*

   In set operations, an inverse element is a set that combined with another given set returns the identity or neutral element corresponding to the operation involved. For the operations studied previously there is not such an inverse element. However, for the symmetric difference, it does exist. Thus, for every set A we can verify that

$$\mathbf{A} \,\Delta\, \mathbf{A} = \varnothing$$

   Since $\varnothing$ is the neutral or identity element for the symmetric difference of sets, then we conclude that the inverse element in this case is the same given set A.

   Proof:

   According to the definition and the results previously shown we know that

$$\begin{aligned} \mathbf{A} \,\Delta\, \mathbf{A} &= (\mathbf{A} \cap \mathbf{A}^c) \cup (\mathbf{A}^c \cap \mathbf{A}) \\ &= \varnothing \cup \varnothing \\ &= \varnothing \end{aligned}$$

   This proves that in fact the inverse element of A is the same A.

Summary of equivalence between languages

Throughout this exposition, we have emphasized the equivalence that exist between the languages of logic and set theory. This does not only provide a clear idea of the importance of logic for mathematical reasoning but also it provides a valuable help in making easier to understand the basic concepts of set theory which are fundamental in building the conceptual body of calculus.

We have seen how each statement of a property or characteristic that becomes a proposition when it is applied to a particular element is associated with a set. Thus, any statement of a tautology in logic is equated with the fact that all elements of a given situation satisfy certain property in set theory. This means that this statement is true for all elements of a given situation. Therefore, we can say that a tautology in logic translates into the universal set in set theory. Likewise, a contradiction translates into an empty set.

We also saw how each logical connective corresponds to either a relationship or to a set operation. We summarize those equivalences in the following table.

Let ***A*** and ***B*** be the sets such that

$$\mathbf{A} = \{x: P(x)\} \qquad \mathbf{B} = \{x: Q(x)\}$$

In SET THEORY	Translates to	PROPOSITIONAL LOGIC
$x \in A$	$\equiv$	$P(x)$
$x \in B$	$\equiv$	$Q(x)$
$x \notin A$	$\equiv$	$\sim P(x)$
$x \notin B$	$\equiv$	$\sim Q(x)$
$A = B$	$\equiv$	$P(x) \Leftrightarrow Q(x)$
$A \subseteq B$	$\equiv$	$P(x) \Rightarrow Q(x)$
A^c	$\equiv$	$\sim P(x)$
B^c	$\equiv$	$\sim Q(x)$
$A \cap B$	$\equiv$	$P(x) \wedge Q(x)$
$A \cup B$	$\equiv$	$P(x) \vee Q(x)$
$A - B$	$\equiv$	$P(x) \wedge \sim Q(x)$
$B - A$	$\equiv$	$\sim P(x) \wedge Q(x)$
$A \Delta B$	$\equiv$	$P(x) \veebar Q(x)$
U	$\equiv$	$P(x) \vee \sim P(x)$
$\varnothing$	$\equiv$	$P(x) \wedge \sim P(x)$

Intersections and unions of family of sets

Both intersection and union of sets can be extended to more than two sets. Let us assume that we have the following set of sets:

$$\{\mathbf{A_1}, \mathbf{A_2}, \cdots, \mathbf{A_n}\}$$

This type of sets is usually called a *family of sets* and we can denote it as follows:

$$\{\mathbf{A_i}\}; \quad i = 1, 2, \cdots, n$$

However, it is very important to mention some issues related to this concept. First, the above definition is not a formal definition of family of sets. A family of sets does not need to be a set itself, since a family of sets allows containing repeated members. For this reason, in some contexts the term "collection" is used, instead.

Second, in formal definitions, this concept is referred to collections of subsets of a given set. For example, suppose that $\boldsymbol{A}$ is a collection of subsets of a given set $\boldsymbol{D}$. In this case we can say that $\boldsymbol{A}$ is a family of sets over $\boldsymbol{D}$. The sets that constitute a family may share some specific characteristics or properties that allow us to identify which subsets of $\boldsymbol{D}$ are members of family $\boldsymbol{A}$.

Third, a family of sets should not be confused with the set of parts that was presented earlier. The set of parts is the set of *all* subsets of a given set, while a family is a particular collection of subsets of that set and it is not necessarily formed by all its subsets. In fact, we can constitute many different families over the same given set. Having said this, let us now proceed with the extension of intersection and union to more than two sets.

Extended intersection and union

The intersection of all sets that form the family given above is

$$\mathbf{A_1} \cap \mathbf{A_2} \cap \cdots \cap \mathbf{A_n}$$

This intersection can be denoted by

$$\bigcap_{i=1}^{n} \mathbf{A_i}$$

The union of the family is

$$\mathbf{A_1} \cup \mathbf{A_2} \cup \cdots \cup \mathbf{A_n}$$

This union can be denoted by

$$\bigcup_{i=1}^{n} A_i$$

Let us consider the following set

$$\mathbf{I_n} = \{1, 2, \cdots, n\}$$

Such that each $\boldsymbol{i} \in \boldsymbol{I_n}$ is associated with a set $\boldsymbol{A_i}$. Thus, we can write both the intersection and the union respectively as follows:

$$\bigcap_{i \in I_n} A_i$$

and

$$\bigcup_{i \in I_n} A_i$$

$\boldsymbol{I_n}$ is usually called the *index set*. Thus, we can say that the set

$$\{\mathbf{A}_i : i \in I_n\}$$

is an *indexed family of sets*.

This way it is easier to present the following definitions:

Given the family:

$$\{A_i: i \in I_n\}$$

The *intersection of the family* is the set

$$\bigcap_{i \in I_n} A_i = \{x: \forall i \in I_n: x \in A_i\}$$

The *union of the family* is the set

$$\bigcup_{i \in I_n} A_i = \{x: \exists i \in I_n: x \in A_i\}$$

The above definitions indicate that the intersection of the family is the set of elements which are members of each set of the family. The union of the family is the set of elements that belong to at least one of the sets of the family.

Properties

The properties that are satisfied by the intersection and union of two sets are also satisfied by these operations extended to more than two sets. We present below the properties that connect both operations.

a) Distributive laws

$$\left(\bigcup_{i \in I_n} A_i\right) \bigcap \left(\bigcup_{j \in I_m} B_j\right) = \bigcup_{\substack{i \in I_n \\ j \in I_m}} \left(A_i \bigcap B_j\right)$$

$$\left(\bigcap_{i \in I_n} A_i\right) \bigcup \left(\bigcap_{j \in I_m} B_j\right) = \bigcap_{\substack{i \in I_n \\ j \in I_m}} \left(A_i \bigcup B_j\right)$$

b) De Morgan law

$$\left(\bigcap_{i\in I_n} A_i\right)^c = \bigcup_{i\in I_n} A_i^c$$

$$\left(\bigcup_{i\in I_n} A_i\right)^c = \bigcap_{i\in I_n} A_i^c$$

PARTITION OF A SET

Given a set $D \neq \varnothing$ and a family A of disjoint and non-empty subsets of D, if the union of all these subsets equals D, then A constitutes a *partition* of D. Formally, the definition is as follows:

Given a set $D \neq \varnothing$ and the family:

$$A = \{A_i : i \in I_n : (A_i \subseteq D) \wedge (A_i \neq \varnothing) \wedge (\forall\, i, j \in I_n : i \neq j : A_i \cap A_j = \varnothing)\}$$

$$A \text{ is a } \textit{partition} \text{ of } D \Leftrightarrow \bigcup_{i\in I_n} A_i = D$$

Example

Let N be the set of natural numbers, E and O the sets of natural even, and odd numbers respectively and the family

$$\{\mathbf{E}, \mathbf{O}\}$$

Since both E and O are non-empty subsets of N and

$$(\mathbf{E} \cap \mathbf{O} = \varnothing) \wedge (\mathbf{E} \cup \mathbf{O} = \mathbf{N})$$

Then, the family $\{\mathbf{E}, \mathbf{O}\}$ is a partition of $\mathbf{N}$.

EXERCISES III

1. Determine the intersection of the given sets and get the corresponding Venn Diagram in each of the following cases:

a) **A** = $\{x: x \in \boldsymbol{N}^* \wedge x \leq 7\}$ **B** = $\{0, 2, 4, 6\}$

b) **C** = $\{x: x \in \boldsymbol{N} \wedge 5 \leq \text{x} \leq 8\}$
D = $\{x: x \in \boldsymbol{N} \wedge x \text{ is even} \wedge x \leq 10\}$

c) **E** = $\{x: x \in \boldsymbol{N} \wedge x \mid 72\}$ **F** = $\{x: x \in \boldsymbol{N} \wedge x \mid 18\}$

2. Verify the commutativity property of intersection of sets using the following pair of sets:

a) **A** = $\{1, 3, 5, 7\}$ **B** = $\{1, 2, 3, 4, 5\}$

b) **C** = $\{x: x \in N \wedge 4 < \text{x} \leq 20\}$ **D** = $\{1, 14, 15, 18, 20\}$

3. Determine the union of the following sets and the corresponding Venn diagram whenever possible:

a) **A** = $\{2, 5, 7\}$ **B** = $\{1, 3, 4, 2\}$

b) **C** = $\{x: x \in \boldsymbol{N} \wedge 4 < \text{x} \leq 20\}$ **D** = $\{1, 14, 15, 18, 20, 25\}$

c) **E** = $\{x: x \in \boldsymbol{N}^* \wedge x < 7\}$ **F** = $\{4, 8, 12\}$

d) **P** = $\{x: x \in \boldsymbol{N} \wedge 4 < x \leq 20\}$
Q = $\{x: x \in \boldsymbol{N} \wedge x \text{ is even} \wedge x < 7\}$

e) **R** = $\{x: x \in \boldsymbol{N} \wedge x > 10\}$ **S** = $\{x: x \in N \wedge 1 < x \leq 7\}$

4. Verify the associative property of union of sets using the following sets:

A = $\{x: x \in \boldsymbol{N} \wedge \wedge x \text{ is odd} \wedge x < 15\}$

B = {1, 2, 3, 4, 5}

C = {x: $x \in \boldsymbol{N} \wedge x$ is even $\wedge\ x \leq 10$}

5. Given the following sets:

   A = {x: $x \in \boldsymbol{N}^* \wedge x < 5$}

   B = {Natural numbers greater than 2 and less than 6}

   C = {x: $x \in \boldsymbol{N} \wedge x$ is odd $\wedge\ 1 \leq x \leq 5$}

   Determine:

$\mathbf{A} \cup \mathbf{B}$	$\mathbf{A} \cup \mathbf{D}$	$\mathbf{B} \cap \mathbf{A}$	$\mathbf{B} \cap \mathbf{C}$
$\mathbf{D} \cap \mathbf{A}$	$\mathbf{B} \cap \mathbf{D}$	$\mathbf{A} \cup \mathbf{C}$	$\mathbf{A} \cap \mathbf{C}$
$\mathbf{B} \cup \mathbf{C}$	$\mathbf{B} \cup \mathbf{D}$	$\mathbf{D} \cup \mathbf{C}$	$\mathbf{C} \cap \mathbf{A}$

6. If $\mathbf{F} \cup \mathbf{G} = \varnothing$, what can we say about **F** and **G**?

7. If $\mathbf{F} \cap \mathbf{G} = \varnothing$, can we conclude that $\mathbf{F} = \varnothing$ or that $\mathbf{G} = \varnothing$?

8. If $\mathbf{F} \subseteq \mathbf{G}$ and $\mathbf{F} \cap \mathbf{G} = \varnothing$, what can we say about **F**?

9. Complete the following propositions:

a) $\mathbf{S} \cap \varnothing =$	*b)* $\varnothing \cup \{0\} =$	*c)* $\mathbf{R} \cap \mathbf{R}^c =$
d) $\mathbf{P} \cup \varnothing =$	*e)* $(\mathbf{P}^c)^c =$	*f)* $\{\varnothing\} \cup \{0\} =$
g) $\varnothing \cap \mathbf{U} =$	*h)* $\{\varnothing\} \cap \{\varnothing\} =$	*i)* $\varnothing \cup \varnothing =$
j) $\varnothing \cap \varnothing^c =$	*k)* $\varnothing \cup \mathbf{U} =$	*l)* $\varnothing \cap \{\varnothing\} =$
m) $\mathbf{K} \cup \mathbf{K}^c =$	*n)* $\varnothing \cap \varnothing =$	

10. Given the following sets:

    A = $\{a, b, c\}$ **B** = $\{a, e, i, o, u\}$

    C = $\{x: x \in N \wedge x \text{ ends in } 7 \wedge x < 28\}$

    D = {3, 5, 7, 8} **P** = {Female students}

    Z = {Married women}

    Determine: **A – B, C – D,** and **P – Z**

11. Use the resulting sets from the previous exercise to verify that the difference of sets does not satisfy the commutative property.

12. Given the sets:

    A = $\{a, b, c, d\}$ **B** = $\{a, b, i\}$ **C** = $\{a, e, i, o\}$ **D** = $\{f, g, c\}$

    Determine:

A – B	**C – D**	**A Δ B**	**A – D**	**B Δ C**
B – C	**D – C**	**D – B**	**B ∪ C**	**C Δ A**
A ∪ B	**C Δ D**	**C ∩ D**	**D ∩ B**	**D – A**

13. According to the Venn diagram given below, determine whether the following propositions are true or false:

    a) $1 \in$ **A – B** *b)* $4 \in$ **A ∪ B** *c)* $5 \in$ **A ∩ B**

    d) $a \in$ **B – A** *e)* $b \in$ **B – A** *f)* **A ∩ B ⊂ A ∪ B**

    g) $8 \in$ **A ∩ B** *h)* **A – B** = $\mathbf{C_A B}$

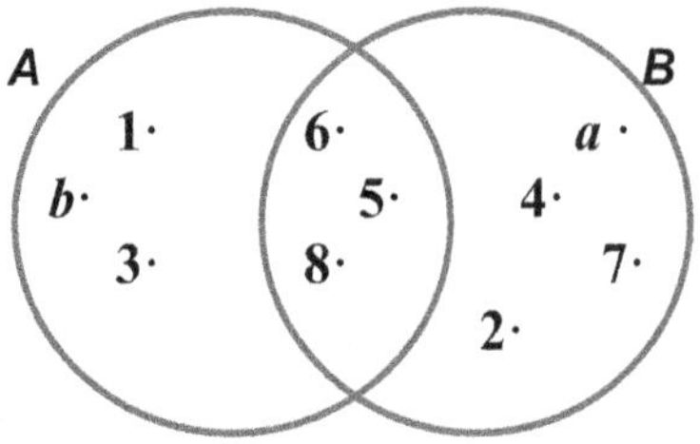

14. Given the following sets:

A = {2, 4, 6, 8}   **B** = {1, 3, 5, 6}   **C** = {2, 3, 4, 5}

Determine:

(A ∪ B) – C	**[(A ∪ C) ∩ B] – (A ∪ B)**
(B ∩ C) – (B ∪ C)	**A ∪ (B – A)**
(A ∩ C) – C	**(B ∩ C) – (A ∪ C)**
(B ∪ C) – (B ∩ C)	**A ∩ (B – A)**

15. Given the sets:

A = $\{x: x \in N \wedge x \text{ is even} \wedge 10 < x < 20\}$

B = $\{x: x \text{ is a divisor of } 12\}$

C = {2, 4}

Determine:

(A – B) ∪ C   **P(C)**   **C$_B$C**   **C – B**

16. Given the sets:

    $\mathbf{A} = \{x: x \in \boldsymbol{Z} \wedge -2 \leq x \leq 2\}$ $\mathbf{B} = \{-3, -2, -1, 0\}$

    $\mathbf{C} = \{x: x \in \boldsymbol{N} \wedge x < 4\}$

    Determine:

    $(\mathbf{B} \cup \mathbf{C}) \cap \mathbf{A}$ $\mathbf{A} \,\Delta\, \mathbf{B}$ $(\mathbf{A} - \mathbf{B}) \cup (\mathbf{B} \cap \mathbf{C})$

17. Given the sets:

    $\mathbf{M} = \{x: x \in \boldsymbol{N}^* \wedge x \text{ is even} \wedge x < 12\}$

    $\mathbf{H} = \{x: x \in \boldsymbol{N} \wedge x \text{ is a divisor of } 4\}$

    $\mathbf{J} = \{2, 4\}$

    Determine:

    $(H - M)$ $P(H)$ $C_M J$

18. By using set notation, write the set that corresponds to the shaded region in each of the following diagrams:

    a)

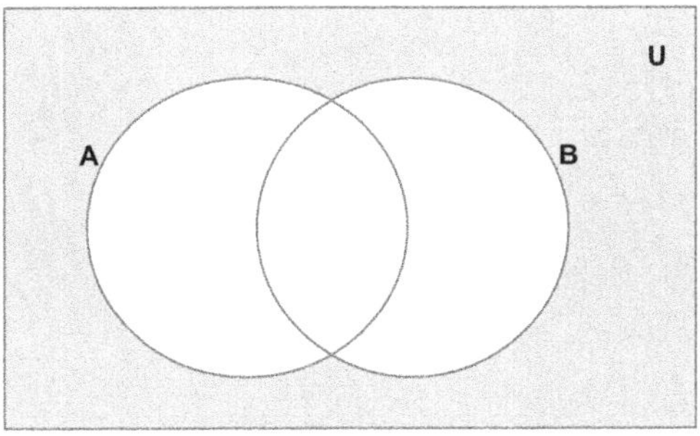

b)

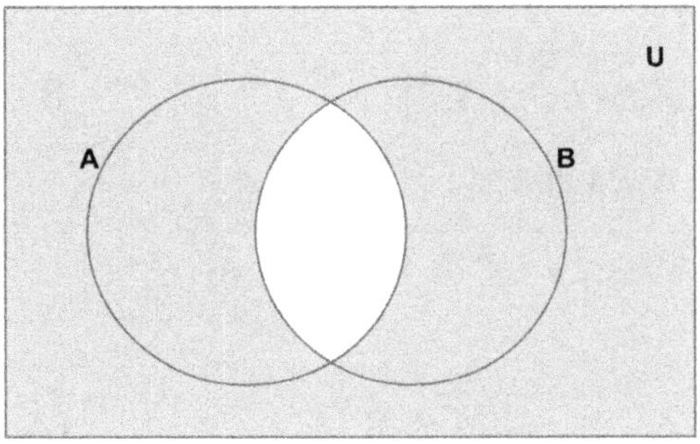

c)

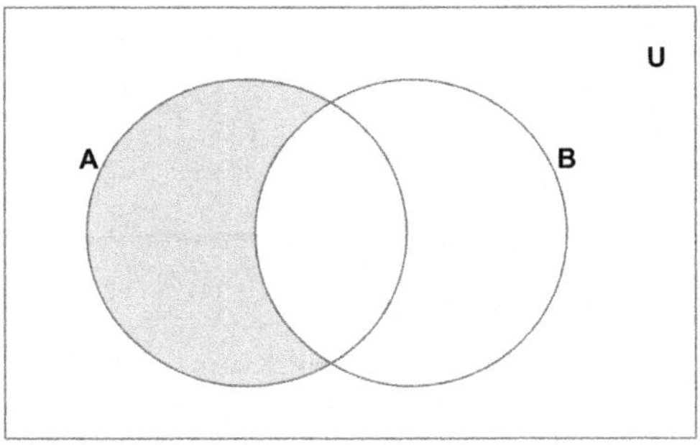

d)

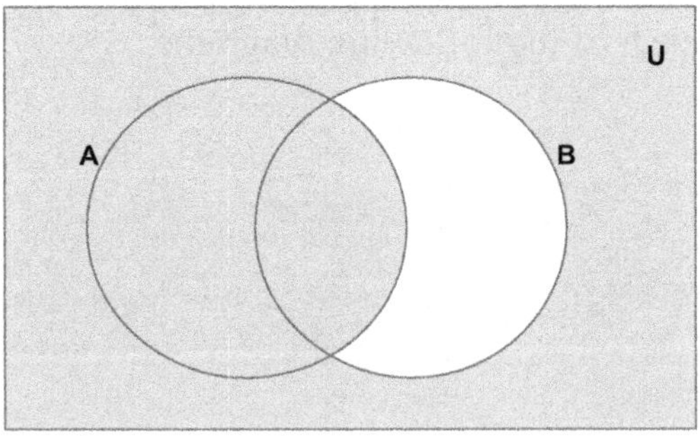

e)

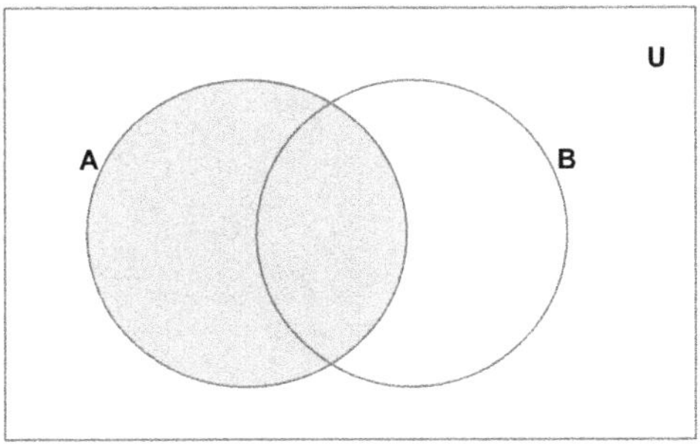

f)

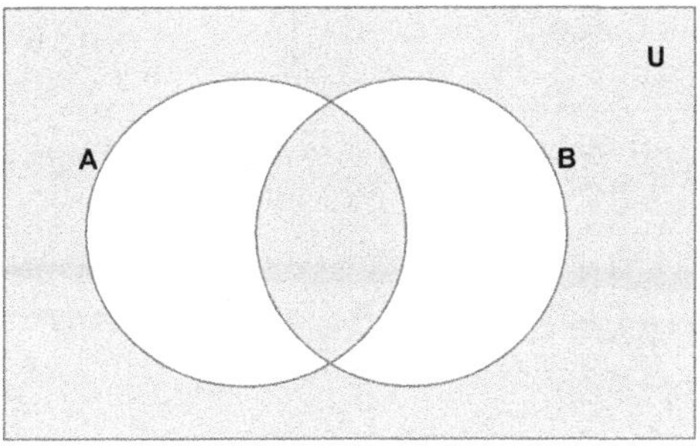

g)

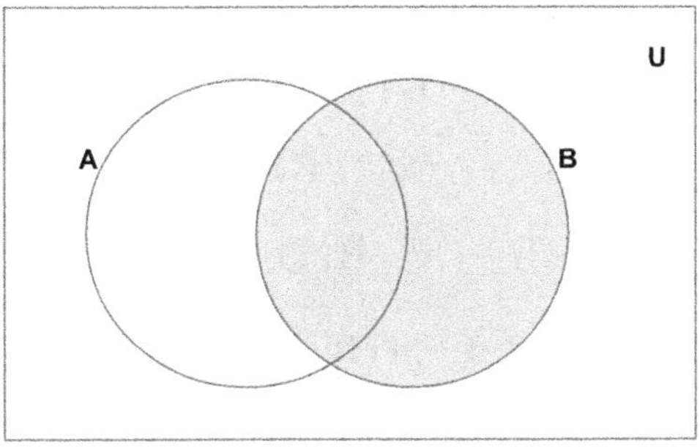

h)

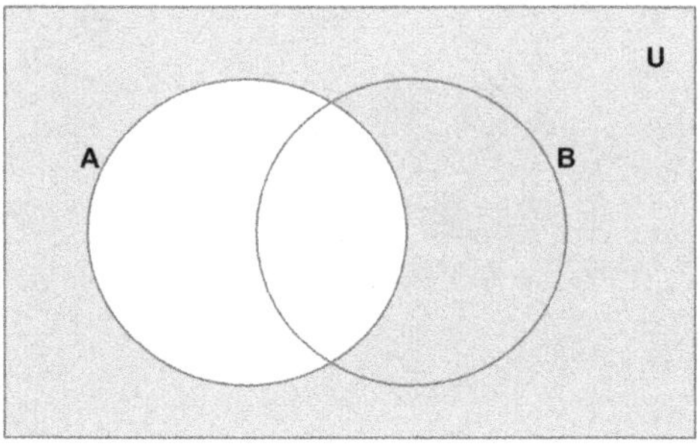

i)

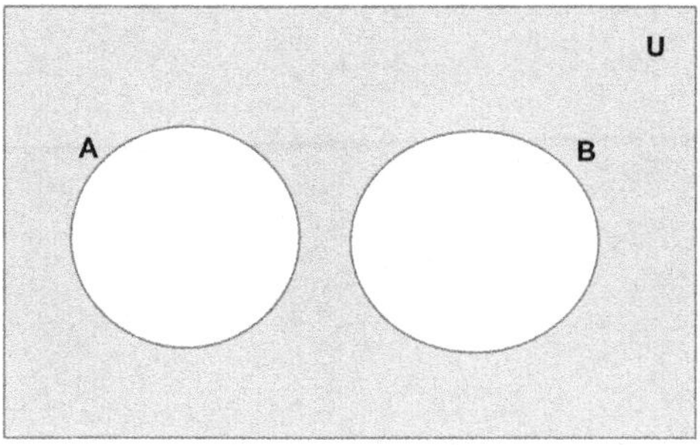

19. By using Venn diagrams, determine which of the following equalities are true:

 a) $\mathbf{A \cap (B \cup C)^c = (B \cap A) \cap C}$

 b) $\mathbf{A \cup (B \cup C)^c = (A^c \cup B)^c \cap (A^c \cap C)^c}$

 c) $\mathbf{A^c - (B \cup C) = (A^c - B) \cup (A^c - C)}$

 d) $\mathbf{A - (B \cup C) = C^c \cap (B^c \cap A)}$

 e) $\mathbf{B \cup (A - C) = (B \cup A) - (B \cup C)}$

f) $\mathbf{A \,\Delta\, B^c = (A \cup B^c) \cap (A^c \cup B)}$

20. Determine whether p is necessary, sufficient, or necessary and sufficient condition for q:

a) p: $\mathbf{A \cap B = A}$
q: $\mathbf{A \subseteq B}$

c) p: $\mathbf{A \subseteq B}$
q: $\mathbf{B^c \subseteq A^c}$

b) p: $\mathbf{(A \cup B) = (A \cap B)}$
q: $\mathbf{A = B}$

d) p: $\mathbf{(A \cap B) \subseteq A}$
q: $\mathbf{A \neq B}$

21. Prove:

a) $\mathbf{[P(A) \cup P(B)] \subseteq P(A \cup B)}$

b) $\mathbf{P(A \cap B) = P(A) \cap P(B)}$

c) $\mathbf{(A \subseteq B) \Leftrightarrow P(A) \subseteq P(B)}$

d) $\mathbf{(A \,\Delta\, B = A \,\Delta\, C) \Rightarrow B = C}$

e) $\mathbf{[(A \,\Delta\, B) \cap C] = [(A \cap C) \,\Delta\, (B \cap C)]}$

22. Given any two non-empty sets A and B, determine which of the following statements are defined and which are not:

a) $\mathbf{C_{A \cap B} A}$

b) $\mathbf{C_{A \cup B} A}$

c) $\mathbf{C_A (A \cap B)}$

d) $\mathbf{C_B (A \cup B)}$

23. Prove:

a) $\mathbf{(B \subseteq A) \Leftrightarrow [(A - B) \cup B = A]}$

b) $\mathbf{A \,\Delta\, U = A^c}$

c) $\mathbf{A} \cap (\mathbf{B} - \mathbf{C}) = [(\mathbf{A} \cap \mathbf{B}) - (\mathbf{A} \cap \mathbf{C})]$

d) $\mathbf{A} \,\Delta\, \mathbf{B} = [(\mathbf{A} \cup \mathbf{B}) \cap (\mathbf{A} \cap \mathbf{B})^{c}]$

e) $\mathbf{A} - \mathbf{B} = \mathbf{B}^{c} - \mathbf{A}^{c}$

f) $[(\mathbf{A} \cup \mathbf{B}) \cap (\mathbf{A}^{c} \cap \mathbf{B}^{c})] = \varnothing$

24. Determine the set of parts of the following sets:

$\mathbf{A} = \{2, \{2, 3\}, \varnothing\}$ $\mathbf{B} = \{\{0\}, 0, \{b\}\}$ $\mathbf{C} = \{1, 2, \{\varnothing\}, a\}$

$\mathbf{D} = \{\varnothing\}$ $\mathbf{E} = \{10\}$ $\mathbf{F} = \{\varnothing, \{\varnothing\}\}$

25. Let **A**, **B**, and **C** be any sets. Since $\mathbf{A} - \mathbf{B} = \mathbf{A} \cap \mathbf{B}^{c}$, prove the following equalities:

a) $\varnothing - \mathbf{A} = \varnothing$

b) $\mathbf{A}^{c} - \mathbf{B}^{c} = \mathbf{B} - \mathbf{A}$

c) $\mathbf{A} - \mathbf{B} = \mathbf{A} - (\mathbf{A} \cap \mathbf{B}) = (\mathbf{A} \cup \mathbf{B}) - \mathbf{B}$

d) $(\mathbf{A} - \mathbf{B}) \cap (\mathbf{B} - \mathbf{A}) = \varnothing$

e) $(\mathbf{A} - \mathbf{B}) - \mathbf{C} = \mathbf{A} - (\mathbf{B} \cup \mathbf{C})$

26. For any set A having a finite number of elements we will denote this number as $n(A)$. Thus, if P and Q are disjoint sets, then

$$n(\mathbf{P} \cup \mathbf{Q}) = n(\mathbf{P}) + n(\mathbf{Q})$$

In general, for any two sets A and B having a finite number of elements it can be verified that

$$n(\mathbf{A} \cup \mathbf{B}) = n(\mathbf{A}) + n(\mathbf{B}) - n(\mathbf{A} \cap \mathbf{B})$$

Given the sets ***A***, ***B***, and ***C*** with a finite number of elements each, derive a formula for

$$n(\mathbf{A} \cup \mathbf{B} \cup \mathbf{C})$$

27. The number of members of clubs ***A*** and ***B*** total 140. Out of the 140 members, 40 belong to both clubs and 60 are members of ***B***. How many members belong to ***A***?

28. The academic registrar reports that there are 200 students from the sciences area enrolled in different courses according to the following distribution: Physics 80, Biology 90, and Chemistry 55. There are 32 students who are enrolled in both Biology and Physics, 23 in both Chemistry and Physics, and 16 in both Biology and Chemistry, while 8 are enrolled in the three courses. Is this report correct?

29. The math teacher gave three tests during the course. At the end of the semester the results were: 2 students failed the three tests, 10 students failed the first and the third test, 9 failed the second and the third test, 5 failed the first and the second test, and 31 failed the first, 26 the second and 31 the third. There were 100 students in this course. How many students passed the three tests?

30. In a town of 1,000 inhabitants, 470 are subscribed to newspaper ***A***, 420 to newspaper ***B***, and 315 to newspaper ***C***. Also, we know that 140 are subscribed to both ***B*** and ***C***, 220 to ***A*** and ***C***, and 110 to ***A*** and ***B***. There are 75 people subscribed to all three newspapers.

    We want to know the following:

    a) How many people are not subscribed to any newspaper?

    b) How many people are subscribed to only two newspapers?

    c) How many people are subscribed to only one newspaper?

31. To know the place of birth, sex, and marital status of government employees, the relevant information was collected from 692 of those employees. They got the following results: 300 males, 230 married, 370 were born in the capital of the country, 150 married males, 180 males were born in the capital, 90 married were born in the capital, and 10 single males were born out of the capital.

We want to know:

a) How many married males were born in the capital?

b) How many married females were born out of the capital?

c) How many single females were born out of the capital?

d) How many people satisfy at least one of the following conditions: married male, male born in the capital, or married and born in the capital?

32. Given the set:

$$\mathbf{A} = \{0, a, -1, +, \varnothing\}$$

Determine whether the following families are a partition of A or not and explain why:

a) $\{\{\varnothing, -1, a\}, \{0, +\}\}$ *b)* $\{\{0, a\}, \{+, -1\}\}$

c) $\{\{0, a, -1, +\}, \varnothing\}$ *d)* $\{\{0\}, \{a\}, \{-1\}, \{+\}, \{\varnothing\}\}$

33. Given the set:

$$\mathbf{A} = \{x: x \in \boldsymbol{Z} \wedge -5 \leq x \leq 5\}$$

Determine whether the following families are a partition of A or not and explain why:

a) $\{\{-5, -4, -3, -2\}, \{-1, 0, 1, 2, 3, 4\}\}$

b) $\{\{-4, -3, -2, -1\}, \{1, 2, 3, 4, 5, -5, 0\}\}$

c) $\{\{x: x \in \mathbf{Z} \wedge x \geq -5\}, \{x: x \in \mathbf{Z} \wedge x \leq 5\}\}$

d) $\{\{x: x \in \mathbf{Z} \wedge -6 < x \leq 0\}, \{x: x \in \mathbf{Z} \wedge 1 \leq x < 6\}\}$

e) $\{\{x: x \in \mathbf{Z} \wedge -5 \leq x \leq -1\}, \{x: x \in \mathbf{Z} \wedge -1 \leq x < 2\},$
$\{x: x \in \mathbf{Z} \wedge 2 \leq x \leq 5\}\}$

NUMBER SETS

We have taken for granted that students have prior knowledge about numerical sets. Therefore, we have already used them in previous examples and proposed exercises. Also, at the beginning of this chapter, we mentioned the existence of different kinds of numbers that are grouped into sets, and their corresponding notations were also introduced. Students beginning their math studies should be able to distinguish and establish the differences between these sets to work with them properly.

Consequently, we need to address in more detail and formality the study of this type of set although without resorting to complex definitions of numbers. We will do this by describing the development of the different number sets as a process stimulated by the need to overcome restrictions. That is, as a process of successive extensions of the numerical sets aimed at solving limitations. Let us start.

The first and the simplest set of numbers that we know is the one used for counting and ordering. Such set is the following:

$$\{1, 2, 3, 4, 5 \ldots\}$$

We denote this set by $\mathbf{N}^*$. Most authors refer to this set as the set of *natural numbers*. There is no consensus on the inclusion or not of the number zero as a natural number. When 0 is added to this set, we get a set of numbers that most authors call the *whole numbers*. However, in this book for simplicity we denote the set of whole numbers by the capital letter $\boldsymbol{N}$ and we refer to it as the set of natural numbers. Thus, we have that

$$\boldsymbol{N} = \{0, 1, 2, 3, 4, 5 \ldots\}$$

What has been said can be schematically represented as:

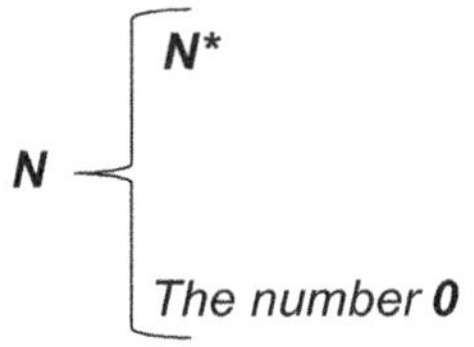

The natural numbers can be ordered from lowest to highest.

The addition and multiplication operations can be fully performed with natural numbers with no restriction. This is, given any two natural numbers, let us say a and b, both

$$a + b \qquad \text{and} \qquad a.b$$

are also natural numbers. By using symbols this is

$$\forall a, b \in \boldsymbol{N}, (a + b) \in \boldsymbol{N} \wedge (a.b) \in \boldsymbol{N}$$

However, the subtraction a - b is not always a natural number. If a is less than b, then $a - b$ is not a natural number. In symbols this is

$$\forall a, b \in \boldsymbol{N}: a < b, (a - b) \notin \boldsymbol{N}$$

Then, we can say that $\boldsymbol{N}$ is closed under the addition and multiplication operations, but it is not under the subtraction operation. In other words, $\boldsymbol{N}$ satisfies the *closure property* under the addition and multiplication operations, but it does not under the subtraction operation.

This limitation raises the need to extend this set by adding the corresponding negative number to each natural number. In this way the set of *integer numbers* is constituted which is denoted by the capital letter $\boldsymbol{Z}$. Thus, we have that

$$\boldsymbol{Z} = \{. . ., -5, -4, -3, -2, -1, 0, 1, 2, 3, 4, 5 . . .\}$$

Schematically, this enlargement process is represented as follows:

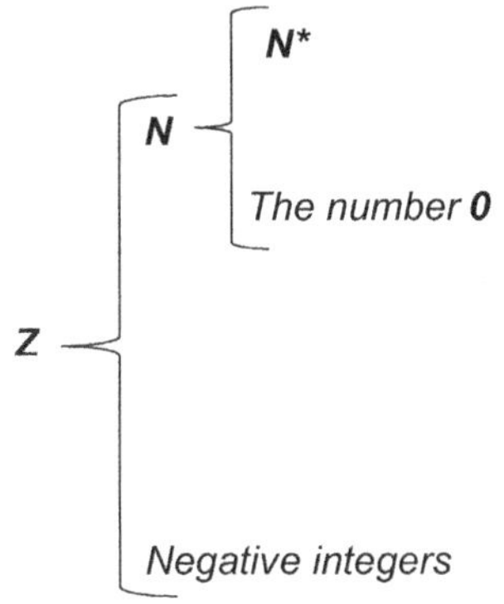

If we wanted to refer to only the positive integers, then we will use the notation $\boldsymbol{Z}^+$. Like natural numbers, integers can also be ordered from lowest to highest. The set $\boldsymbol{Z}$ is closed under the addition, the multiplication, and the subtraction operations. By using symbols this is

$$\forall a, b \in \boldsymbol{Z}, (a + b) \in \boldsymbol{Z} \wedge (a - b) \in \boldsymbol{Z} \wedge (a.b) \in \boldsymbol{Z}$$

However, $\boldsymbol{Z}$ does not satisfy the closure property under the division operation. In fact, being a and b any two integer numbers such that a is not a multiple of b the quotient a/b is not an integer. Again, this limitation raises the need for another extension of the set of numbers which consists in adding the *fractional numbers*. In this way, we constitute the set of *rational numbers* which is denoted by the capital letter $\boldsymbol{Q}$. Therefore, the closure property is satisfied by $\boldsymbol{Q}$ under the addition, the subtraction, the multiplication, and the division operations. In symbols this is

$$\forall a, b \in \boldsymbol{Q}, (a + b) \in \boldsymbol{Q} \wedge (a - b) \in \boldsymbol{Q} \wedge (a.b) \in \boldsymbol{Q} \wedge (a/b) \in \boldsymbol{Q}$$

Like natural and integer numbers, the rational numbers can also be ordered from lowest to highest.

The density property

There is an important property satisfied by $\boldsymbol{Q}$ that distinguishes this set from the previous ones. This is the *density property*. This property tells us that there always exists another rational number that lies between any two given rational numbers no matter how close they are to each other. This property implies that between any two rational numbers there is always an infinite number of rational numbers no matter how close these two numbers are to each other.

Because of this property, it is not possible to describe by extension a subset of $\boldsymbol{Q}$ that is constituted by all rational numbers that lie between any two given rational numbers as we have done with similar subsets of either $\boldsymbol{N}$ or $\boldsymbol{Z}$. Therefore, a formal definition for $\boldsymbol{Q}$ is needed.

For this purpose, we must state first that a given number is a rational number, if and only if, it can be expressed by the quotient of two integer numbers. This definition of a rational number allows us to provide the following formal description by comprehension of $\boldsymbol{Q}$:

$$Q = \{x: \exists\ a,\ b \in Z \wedge b \neq 0: x = a/b\}$$

The above definition states that a number x is a rational number, if and only if, there are two integers a and b such that $x = a/b$ being $b \neq 0$. Thus, once the fractional numbers are added, the expansion process of numbers schematically represented looks as follows:

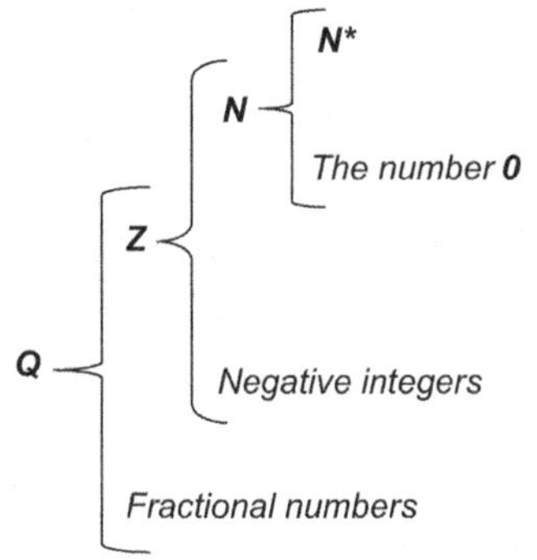

To understand the need for an additional extension of the set of numbers, it is useful to devote some time by considering the representation of rational numbers as points on a straight line.

The number line

In mathematics, graphic representations are of great help. These representations allow visualizing concepts what makes it easier to understand them. For example, this is the role played by Venn diagrams in set theory. In the case of numbers, the representation consists of associating points on a straight line with rational numbers according to the following procedure:

1) We take any point on a straight line which is identified by the capital letter O. We call this point "Origin". The rational 0 (zero) is associated with this point which divides the straight line into two half-lines. The negative rational numbers are represented by points on the straight line lying to the left side of O while the positive numbers are represented by points lying to the right side of O (See Figure 2.11).

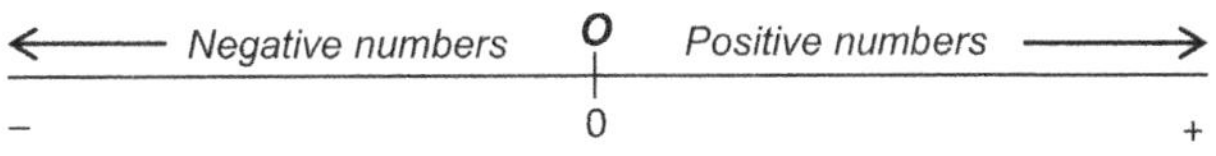

Figure 2.11

2) Let us now locate another point to the right side of O which is identified by the capital letter U. The rational number 1 (one) is associated with this point. Thus, the length of the $\overline{OU}$ segment is taken as the unit of measure to represent any rational number by a point on the straight line (See Figure 2.12).

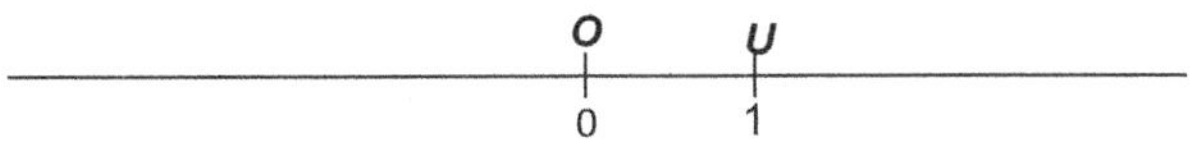

Figure 2.12

3) To represent any positive integer all we need to do is to move from O the $\overline{OU}$ segment as many times as the value of the given number to the right of O. If the number is a negative integer, we must do the same to the left side of O. By following this procedure, we have represented the integers 3 and -2 in Figure 2.13 associated with the points identified by the capital letters ***A*** and ***B*** respectively. We got point ***A*** moving the $\overline{OU}$ segment three times from O to the right and point ***B*** moving the $\overline{OU}$ segment two times from O to the left.

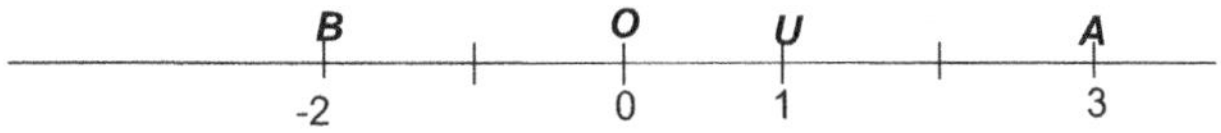

Figure 2.13

4) To represent fractional numbers such as m/n (m and n integer numbers), we divide the $\overline{OU}$ segment into n equal parts. Then, we move the nth part m times from O either to the right if it is a positive number or to the left if it is a negative number. By applying this method, we have represented the fractional number 5/3 in Figure 2.14 associated with the point identified by the capital letter C. We divided the $\overline{OU}$ segment into three equal parts (each one of length 1/3) and moved the 3th part 5 times from O to the right to get point C.

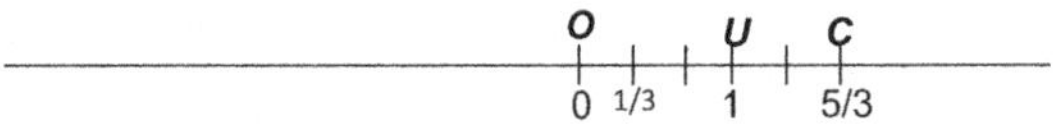

Figure 2.14

By following the procedure described above, it is possible to represent any rational number on the number line. That is to say that *all* rational numbers can be associated to a point on the number line. However, *not all* points on the number line can be associated with a rational number. This means that there are points on the number line for which it is not possible to find a rational number to associate with. A classic example is depicted in Figure 2.15.

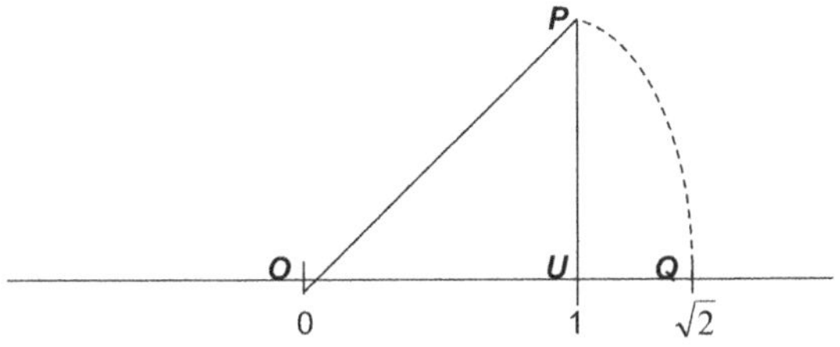

Figure 2.15

In Figure 2.15, the $\overline{OP}$ segment is the hypotenuse of a right triangle with the other two sides of length equal to unity. According to the Pythagoras's theorem, the length of the $\overline{OP}$ segment equals $\sqrt{2}$. Therefore, the point that we have located on the number line which is identified by the capital letter Q must be associated with the number $\sqrt{2}$. The problem is that there is not any rational number whose square is equal to 2. This means that there is not any rational number that measures the length of the $\overline{OQ}$ segment.

$\sqrt{2}$ is not a rational number

Given the relevance of this finding, we need to prove that in fact there is not any rational number whose square equals to 2. Before doing this, we need to recall the following facts that we have used previously:

1) All integer numbers can be written as either $2k$ or $2k + 1$, being k some other integer. Those integers written as $2k$ are even numbers while those written as $2k + 1$ are odd numbers.

2) Also, we proved earlier in Chapter 1 that squares of even numbers are even while squares of odd numbers are odd. The respective converse forms are also true.

The easiest way of proving that $\sqrt{2}$ is not a rational number is by applying the contradiction or reduction to absurdity method that we learnt in Chapter 1. To apply this method, we must start by assuming as a premise the negation of the given statement. Therefore, our premise will be that $\sqrt{2}$ is a rational number. Thus, according to the definition of a rational number given earlier, we must start by assuming that in fact there exist the integers a and b such that

$$(a/b)^2 = 2$$

Also, we assume that a and b have no common factor. This assumption does not raise any additional restriction on the number, since we could simplify it until all common divisors are eliminated. This means that any rational number can be written as a/b being a and b integers with no common factor. Therefore, we can proceed as follows:

$[\exists\, a, b \in \boldsymbol{Z}: (a/b)^2 = 2] \wedge [\nexists\, c \in \boldsymbol{Z}: (c \mid a) \wedge (c \mid b)]$

$[\exists\, a, b \in \boldsymbol{Z}: (a/b)^2 = 2] \wedge [\nexists\, c \in \boldsymbol{Z}: (c \mid a) \wedge (c \mid b)] \quad \Rightarrow a^2 = 2b^2$

$(a^2 = 2b^2) \quad \Rightarrow a^2 \text{ is even}$

$(a^2 \text{ is even}) \quad \Rightarrow a \text{ is even}$

$(a \text{ is even}) \quad \Rightarrow \exists\, 2: 2 \mid a$

$(\exists\, 2: 2 \mid a) \quad \Rightarrow \exists\, k \in \boldsymbol{Z}: a = 2k$

$(a = 2k) \quad \Rightarrow a^2 = 4k^2$

$(a^2 = 4k^2) \quad \Rightarrow 4k^2 = 2b^2$ From premise $(a/b)^2 = 2$

$(4k^2 = 2b^2) \quad \Rightarrow b^2 = 2k^2$

$(b^2 = 2k^2) \quad \Rightarrow b^2 \text{ is even}$

$(b^2 \text{ is even}) \quad \Rightarrow b \text{ is even}$

$(b \text{ is even}) \quad \Rightarrow \exists\, 2: 2 \mid b$

$\therefore \exists\, 2: (2 \mid a) \wedge (2 \mid b)$

This conclusion contradicts the following premise:

$$\nexists\, c \in \boldsymbol{Z}: (c \mid a) \wedge (c \mid b)$$

This proves that in fact there is not any rational number whose square equals 2. Consequently, it has been proven that there exists a point on the number line to which it is not possible to associate any rational number. Furthermore, there are infinite points that lie between any other two points on the number line with which it is not possible to associate any rational number.

The set of real numbers

To be able to associate each point on the number line with a number raises the need for another extension of the number set to include numbers that can be associated with those points for which there are not rational numbers available. Such numbers are known as *irrationals* and their union with the rational numbers gives rise to the set of *real numbers* which is denoted by the capital letter ***R***. In this way, all points on the number line can be associated with a *real number* and vice versa.

Like the rational numbers the real numbers can be ordered from lowest to highest and they also satisfy the density property.

The real number that is associated with a point on the number line is known as the *coordinate* of that point. For instance, in figures 2.13-15 the real numbers -2, 0, 1, 5/3, 3, and $\sqrt{2}$ are the coordinates of points *B*, *O*, *U*, *C*, *A*, and *Q* respectively.

This association of real numbers with points on the number line is helpful to visualize the relationship "less than" that can be established between real numbers. Thus, given any two real numbers *a* and *b*, if *a* is less than *b*, then *a* is associated with a point located on the number line to the left side of the point associated with *b* (See Figure 2.16).

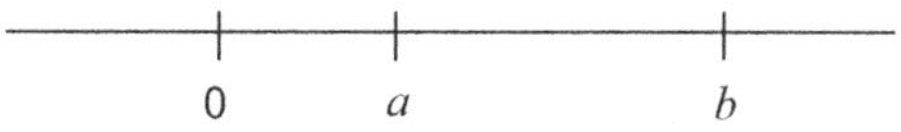

Figure 2.16

For example, the real numbers represented in Figure 2.13 satisfy:

$$-2 < 0 < 1 < 3$$

These numbers are associated with the points ***B***, ***O***, ***U***, and ***A*** on the number line, respectively. We can also see that each point is located to the left of the next according to the relationship "less than". In general, considering real numbers from lowest to highest implies moving from left to right on the number line.

When we want to refer to *all* real numbers that lie between any other two given real numbers a and b such that $a < b$, as depicted in Figure 2.16, we usually write

$$a < x < b$$

We will be back to this subject when considering the concept of "intervals of real numbers" in the next section.

So far, the expansion process of the numerical sets looks schematically as follows:

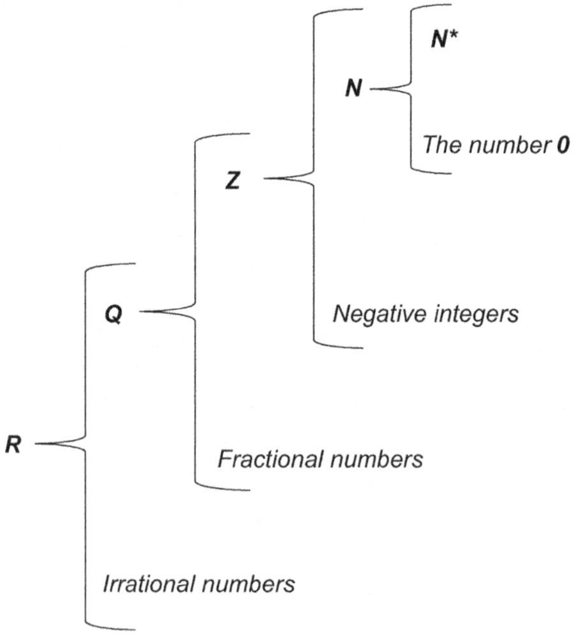

Imaginary numbers

There is still one limitation when working with the set ***R***. For example, let us have the following equation:

$$x^2 + 4 = 0$$

The solution of this equation is

$$x = \sqrt{-4}$$

The problem is that there is not any real number whose square equals -4. The square of any positive or negative number is always a positive number. Therefore, there is no way for the square of any real number to equal a negative one. In fact, there are infinite situations like the one that emerged from the equation shown above. For example, a more general equation would be the following:

$$x^2 + a = 0$$

Where a is any real number such that $a > 0$.

Getting back to the previous equation, to get a solution we need to do the following:

$$x = \sqrt{4(-1)} = \sqrt{4}\sqrt{-1} = \pm 2\sqrt{-1}$$

If we do $i = \sqrt{-1}$, then the solutions are $2i$ and $-2i$ which are not real numbers. In the case of the more general example given above the solutions are:

$$x = \sqrt{a(-1)} = \sqrt{a}\sqrt{-1} = \pm\left(\sqrt{a}\right)i$$

These numbers are called *imaginary* numbers.

The imaginary numbers are part of a wider system of numbers called *complex numbers*. The general form of a complex number is as follows:

$$a + bi$$

Where a represents the *real part* of the number and bi is the *imaginary part*. Any complex number for which $b = 0$ is a real number, while those for which $a = 0$ are imaginary numbers. This means that all real numbers are also complex numbers. The set of complex numbers is denoted by the capital letter ***C***. Then, it is verified that

$$\boldsymbol{R} \subset \boldsymbol{C}$$

Therefore, the different sets of numbers that have been developed satisfy the inclusion relationship as follows:

$$\boldsymbol{N}^* \subset \boldsymbol{N} \subset \boldsymbol{Z} \subset \boldsymbol{Q} \subset \boldsymbol{R} \subset \boldsymbol{C}$$

From now on our study will be framed in the context of real numbers.

Intervals

Intervals are subsets of ***R*** of very frequent use in Mathematics. They are infinite sets of consecutive real numbers that lie between two other given real numbers.

For example, the set of all consecutive real numbers lying between 2 and 5 constitutes an interval. In general, given any two real numbers a and b such that $a < b$, all consecutive real numbers lying between a and b constitute an interval. The numbers a and b are known as the *endpoints* of the interval, being a the lower end and b the upper end.

Intervals can be classified according to whether the endpoints belong to the considered interval or not as follows:

1) *Open Interval*

   The endpoints are not included as members of the interval. Such interval is denoted (a, b) and can be described by comprehension as follows:

$$(a, b) = \{x: x \in \boldsymbol{R} \wedge a < x < b\}$$

One way of illustrating an open interval on the number line is shown in Figure 2.17.

Figure 2.17

2) *Closed Interval*

The endpoints are included as members of the interval. Such interval is denoted $[a, b]$ and can be described by comprehension as follows:

$$[a, b] = \{x: x \in \boldsymbol{R} \wedge a \leq x \leq b\}$$

One way of illustrating a closed interval on the number line is shown in Figure 2.18.

Figure 2.18

3) *Half-Open (Closed) Interval*

One endpoint is included but not the other. Depending on which endpoint is included they can be denoted either $(a, b]$ or $[a, b)$. The respective descriptions by comprehension are as follows:

$$(a, b] = \{x: x \in \boldsymbol{R} \wedge a < x \leq b\}$$

$$[a, b) = \{x: x \in \boldsymbol{R} \wedge a \leq x < b\}$$

Figure 2.19 provides the respective illustrations.

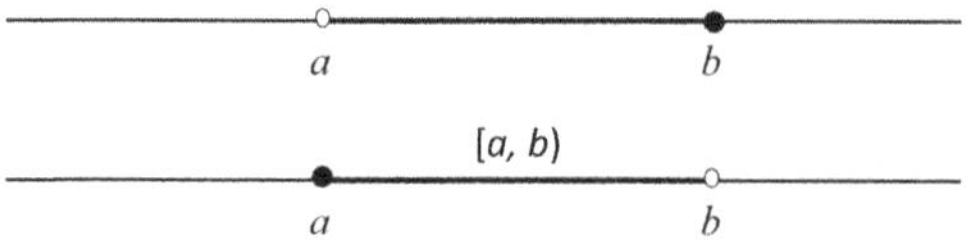

Figure 2.19

4) *Intervals with an infinite endpoint*

Intervals with an infinite endpoint are those intervals that have not bound in the respective direction. The notations and descriptions for this type of intervals are as follows:

$$(a, \infty) = \{x: x \in \boldsymbol{R} \wedge x > a\}$$

$$[a, \infty) = \{x: x \in \boldsymbol{R} \wedge x \geq a\}$$

$$(-\infty, b) = \{x: x \in \boldsymbol{R} \wedge x < b\}$$

$$(-\infty, b] = \{x: x \in \boldsymbol{R} \wedge x \leq b\}$$

The symbols $-\infty$ and ∞ are read "minus infinity" (or "negative infinity") and "infinity" respectively. These symbols are used to represent the unbounded endpoints of the interval.

The $-\infty$ is used for the lower end (left direction on the number line) and ∞ for the upper end (right direction on the number line). They are not real numbers. For this reason, it does not make any sense to write either $(a, \infty]$ or $x \leq \infty$ because there is not a real number x such that $x = \infty$.

The set of all real numbers sometimes is written as an interval with both endpoints unbounded. This is $\boldsymbol{R} = (-\infty, \infty)$.

Figure 2.20 provides illustrations of intervals with infinite endpoints.

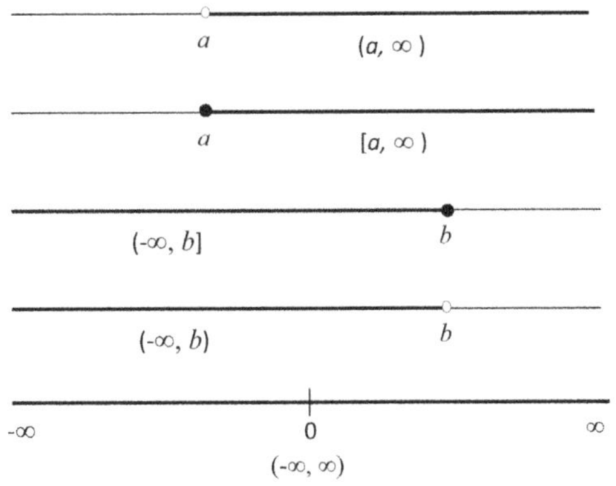

Figure 2.20

All the operations and the relationships that were previously defined for sets are of course satisfied by intervals.

Examples

1) Given the following intervals:

A = [-4, 1) **B** = (-3, 2] **C** = [1, 3]

Determine:

a) $\mathbf{A} \cup \mathbf{B}$ *b)* $\mathbf{A} \cap \mathbf{B}$ *c)* $\mathbf{A} \cap \mathbf{C}$

d) $\mathbf{C} - \mathbf{B}$ *e)* $\mathbf{A}^c$ *f)* $(\mathbf{A} \cap \mathbf{C})^c$

Solutions:

a) [-4, 2] *b)* (-3, 1) *c)* ∅

d) (2, 3] *e)* (-∞, -4) ∪ [1, ∞) *f)* ***R***

Let us have a closer look at cases *a)* and *b)* to explain the procedure we followed and the reasoning:

For case *a)*, we represent intervals ***A*** and ***B*** on two separated number lines by using the same unitary segment and by making the origin of both lines match as shown in Figure 2.21.

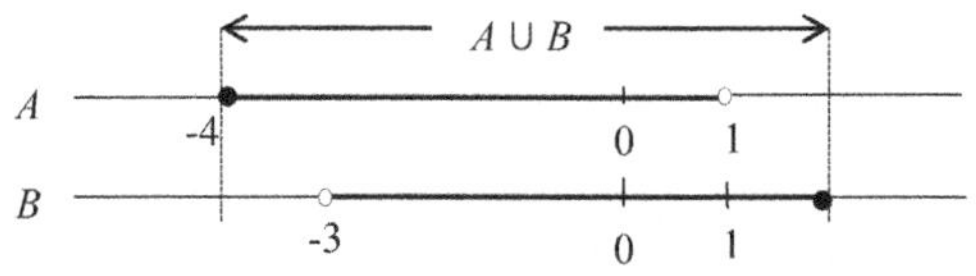

Figure 2.21

The exercise seeks to determine the union of intervals ***A*** and ***B***. Then, according to the definition, an element belongs to the union of two sets, if and only if, it belongs to at least one of them. In this case, this means that the union is the interval formed by all real numbers of both intervals taken altogether. The result includes both endpoints -4 and 2, since -4 is included in ***A*** while 2 is included in ***B***. Thus, the solution is the closed interval [-4, 2].

In the case *b)*, the exercise seeks to determine the intersection of ***A*** and ***B***. The resulting interval is then constituted by only the common real numbers of the two given intervals as shown in Figure 2.22.

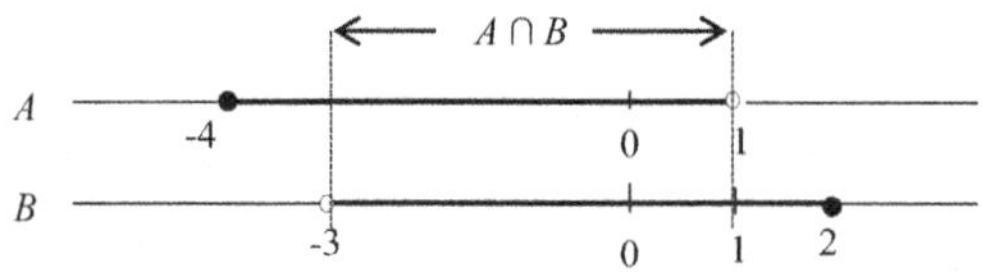

Figure 2.22

The lower endpoint of $\boldsymbol{B}$ belongs to A but not to $\boldsymbol{B}$, therefore it is not included in the resulting intersection. Likewise, the upper endpoint of $\boldsymbol{A}$ belongs to $\boldsymbol{B}$ but not to A and consequently it does not belong to the resulting intersection. Thus, the result of this exercise is the open interval (-3, 1).

2) Given the interval:

$$\mathbf{A} = (-2, 7]$$

Determine whether the family:

$$\{\mathbf{A_1}, \mathbf{A_2}, \mathbf{A_3}\}$$

constitutes a partition of the interval A in the cases *a)*, *b)*, and *c)* given below:

a) $\mathbf{A_1} = (-2, 0)$ $\mathbf{A_2} = [0, 4)$ $\mathbf{A_3} = [4, \infty)$

This family does not constitute a partition of interval A because A_3 is not a subset of A and therefore

$$\mathbf{A_1} \cup \mathbf{A_2} \cup \mathbf{A_3} = (-2, \infty) \neq \mathbf{A}$$

b) $\mathbf{A_1} = (-2, 0]$ $\mathbf{A_2} = (0, 2)$ $\mathbf{A_3} = [2, 7]$

This family constitutes a partition of interval A because

$$\mathbf{A_1} \cup \mathbf{A_2} \cup \mathbf{A_3} = \mathbf{A}$$

and

$$\mathbf{A_1} \cap \mathbf{A_2} = \mathbf{A_1} \cap \mathbf{A_3} = \mathbf{A_2} \cap \mathbf{A_3} = \varnothing$$

c) $\mathbf{A_1} = (-2, 1]$ $\mathbf{A_2} = (1, 3]$ $\mathbf{A_3} = [3, 7]$

This family does not constitute a partition of interval A because

$$\mathbf{A_2} \cap \mathbf{A_3} = \{3\} \neq \varnothing$$

EXERCISES IV

1. Determine whether the following propositions are true or false:

a) $3 \in \boldsymbol{R}$ *b)* $2\pi \in \boldsymbol{Q}$ *c)* $-6 \in \boldsymbol{Q}$ *d)* $\pi \in R$

e) $\sqrt{\frac{4}{25}} \in R$ *f)* $-1 \in \boldsymbol{Q}$ *g)* $\sqrt{16} \in N$ *h)* $3 \in Z$

i) $\sqrt{-7} \in \boldsymbol{Q}$ j) $\sqrt{-16} \in \boldsymbol{R}$ *k)* $\pi \in Q$ *l)* $9 \in N$

m) $-8 \notin \boldsymbol{Z}$ *n)* $\sqrt{3} \notin \boldsymbol{Q}$ *o)* $7/3 \notin \boldsymbol{Q}$ *p)* $0 \in \boldsymbol{Q}$

q) $-3 \notin N$ *r)* $2/3 \in \boldsymbol{Z}$ *s)* $1/3 \in \boldsymbol{Z}$ *t)* $-1 \in N$

2. Describe by comprehension the following intervals:

A = [-3, 5) **B** = (4, 10) **C** = [0, 7] **D** = (-5, 3]

E = [-7, -2) **F** = (0, 4) **G** = [-3, -2) **H** = (-2, 8]

I = (2, 5] **J** = [-3, 0]

3. Given the sets below, represent them on the number line and then describe them by using the interval notation:

A = $\{x: x \in \boldsymbol{R} \wedge x < 3\}$ **B** = $\{x: x \in \boldsymbol{R} \wedge x > -2\}$

C = $\{x: x \in \boldsymbol{R} \wedge x \geq -5\}$ **D** = $\{x: x \in \boldsymbol{R} \wedge x \leq 7\}$

E = $\{x: x \in \boldsymbol{R} \wedge 0 < x \leq 3\}$ **F** = $\{x: x \in \boldsymbol{R} \wedge x \geq 3\}$

G = $\{x: x \in \boldsymbol{R} \wedge -3 \leq x \leq 3\}$ **H** = $\{x: x \in \boldsymbol{R} \wedge -1/2 \leq x > \sqrt{2}\}$

I = $\{x: x \in \boldsymbol{R} \wedge -1 < x < 3\}$

4. Given the intervals:

$\mathbf{A} = [-4, 1/2)$ $\mathbf{B} = (-1, 3/2)$ $\mathbf{C} = (-\infty, 1]$

Determine:

a) $\mathbf{A} \cup \mathbf{B}$ *b)* $\mathbf{A} - \mathbf{B}$ *c)* $\mathbf{A} - \mathbf{C}$ *d)* $\mathbf{B} \cup \mathbf{C}$

e) $\mathbf{B} - \mathbf{C}$ *f)* $\mathbf{A} \cap \mathbf{B}$ *g)* $\mathbf{B} - \mathbf{A}$ *h)* $\mathbf{A} \cap \mathbf{C}$

i) $\mathbf{C} - \mathbf{A}$ *j)* $\mathbf{B} \cap \mathbf{C}$ *k)* $\mathbf{C} - \mathbf{B}$ *l)* $\mathbf{A} \Delta \mathbf{B}$

m) $\mathbf{A} \Delta \mathbf{C}$ *n)* $\mathbf{B} \Delta \mathbf{C}$ *o)* $\mathbf{A} \cup \mathbf{C}$

5. Perform the operations indicated below and graphically represent the resulting interval of each case:

a) $[-2, 8) - [-2, 2]^c$ *b)* $\{[-3, 4) - (0, 5)\}^c$

c) $\{[-3, 5] \cap [0, 6)\}^c$ *d)* $\{(-\infty, 4) \cup (-2, 7]\}^c$

e) $[3, 5)^c - [0, 4)$ *f)* $[-3, 2) \cap (0, 5]$

g) $\{[-1, 2) \cup (0, 3]\}^c$ *h)* $\{[-3, 6) - [-2, 7]\}^c$

i) $\{[-8, 7] \cap (2, 9)\} - (-\infty, 4)^c$ *j)* $(-5, 3] \cap [-8, 0)^c$

6. Given the sets:

$\mathbf{A} = \{x\text{: } x \in \boldsymbol{R} \wedge x - ½ \leq 2\}$ $\mathbf{B} = \{x\text{: } x \in \boldsymbol{R} \wedge -3x - 2 < 1\}$

Determine the following sets and write the solution by using interval notation for those which are not empty sets:

a) $\mathbf{A} \cap \mathbf{B}$ *b)* $\mathbf{A}^c$ *c)* $\mathbf{A} - \mathbf{B}$ *d)* $(\mathbf{A} - \mathbf{B}) \cup (\mathbf{B} - \mathbf{A})$
e) $\mathbf{A} \cup \mathbf{B}$ *f)* $\mathbf{B}^c$ *g)* $\mathbf{B} - \mathbf{A}$ *h)* $\mathbf{A} \Delta \mathbf{B}$

7. Given the interval:

$$(-15, 17]$$

Determine whether the family of intervals:

$$\{A_1, A_2, A_3, A_4, A_5\}$$

constitutes a partition of the given interval above for each of the following cases:

a) $A_1 = (-15, -10)$ $A_2 = [-10, -5]$ $A_3 = (-5, 5)$ $A_4 = [5, 10]$
$A_5 = (10, 17]$

b) $A_1 = (-15, -10)$ $A_2 = (-10, -5]$ $A_3 = (-5, 5)$ $A_4 = [5, 10]$
$A_5 = (10, 17]$

c) $A_1 = (-15, -5)$ $A_2 = (-15, -10)$ $A_3 = (-5, 0)$ $A_4 = [5, 10]$
$A_5 = (0, 10]$

d) $A_1 = (-15, -2)$ $A_2 = [-2, 10)$ $A_3 = [10, 12]$ $A_4 = (12, 16]$
$A_5 = (16, 17]$

e) $A_1 = [-15, -2)$ $A_2 = [-2, 10)$ $A_3 = [10, 12]$ $A_4 = (12, 16]$
$A_5 = (16, 17]$

f) $A_1 = (-15, -10]$ $A_2 = (-10, -5]$ $A_3 = (-5, 5)$ $A_4 = [5, 10]$
$A_5 = (10, 17]$

8. Determine which of the following families are partitions of *R*:

{***Z***, {*Fractional numbers*}}

{***Q***, {*Irrational numbers*}}

{*Even numbers*}, {*Odd numbers*}, ***Q***, {*Irrational numbers*}}

{***Q***, {Irrational numbers}, {*Imaginary numbers*}}

{*N*, ***Z***, ***Q***, {*Irrational numbers*}}

{***Q***, {*Irrational numbers*}, ∅}

{***Z***, {*Fractional numbers*}, ***Q***, {*Irrational numbers*}}

{***Z***, {*Fractional numbers*}, {*Irrational numbers*}}

{{0}, $\boldsymbol{Z}^+$, {*Negative Integer numbers*}, {*Fractional numbers*}, {*Irrational numbers*}}

ANSWERS TO THE EXERSICES PROPOSED IN CHAPTER 2

EXERCISES I

1. **A** = {1, 3, 5, 7, 9} **B** = {2, 4, 6, 8, 10} **C** = {-2, -1,0, 1, 2, 3}

   D = {3, 5, 7, 9} **E** = ∅ **F** = {1, 2, 3, 4, 5, 5, 7, 8, 9}

2. *a)* F *b)* T *c)* F *d)* T *e)* F *f)* T

3.
a) **A** is the set of natural numbers less than or equal to six.

b) **B** is the set of all rational numbers such that added to ½ the result is a natural number.

c) **C** is the set of natural numbers such that multiplied by 4 minus 6 are greater than or equal to 5 and less than or equal to 30.

d) **H** is the set of lines in the plane that are parallel to line *a*.

e) **M** is the set of lines in the plane that are perpendicular to line *a*.

f) **E** is the set of natural umbers such that multiplied by 2 minus 3 are greater than 2 and less than or equal to 11.

g) **F** is the set of natural numbers that are not members of *E*.

4.
a) $\{x: x = 2n \wedge n \in \boldsymbol{N}\}$

b) $\{x: x \in \boldsymbol{R} \wedge x^3 - 2x^2 - x + 2 = 0\}$

c) $\{x: x \in \boldsymbol{N} \wedge -16 < 10x - 78 \leq 3\}$

5. $\mathbf{A} = \{x: x = 2n + 1 \land n \in \boldsymbol{N} \land n \leq 7\}$ or

$\mathbf{A} = \{x: x = 2n + 1 \land n \in \boldsymbol{N} \land x \leq 15\}$

$\mathbf{B} = \{x: x = n^2 \land n \in \boldsymbol{N}^* \land n \leq 6\}$

$\mathbf{C} = \{x: x \in \boldsymbol{N} \land x \text{ is a prime number} \land n \leq 7\}$

$\mathbf{D} = \{x: x = 2^n \land n \in \boldsymbol{N} \land n \leq 6\}$

6. No, because **C** is a set of sets.

7. **A** y **C**.

EXERCISES II

1. *a)* Yes *b)* Yes *c)* No

2. *a)* F *b)* F *c)* F *d)* F *e)* F *f)* T

3. $\mathbf{B} \subset \mathbf{A}$ $\mathbf{D} \subset \mathbf{A}$ $\mathbf{D} \subset \mathbf{C}$

4.

a)

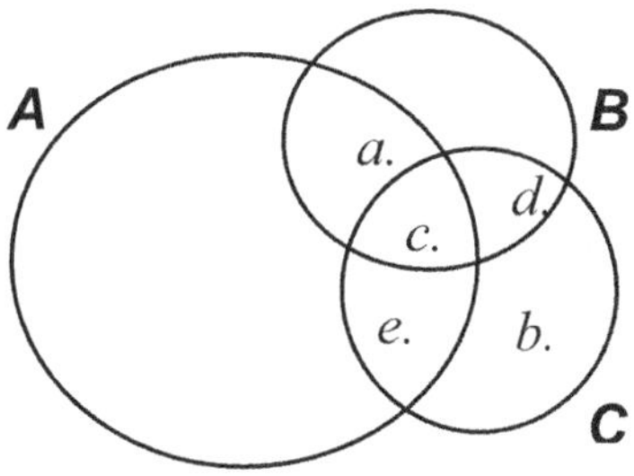

b)

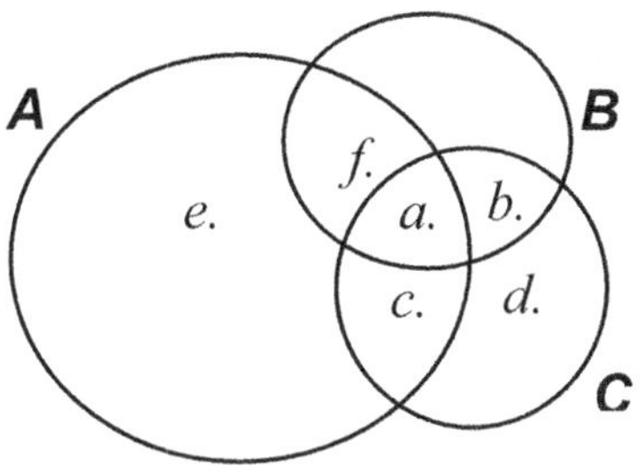

c)

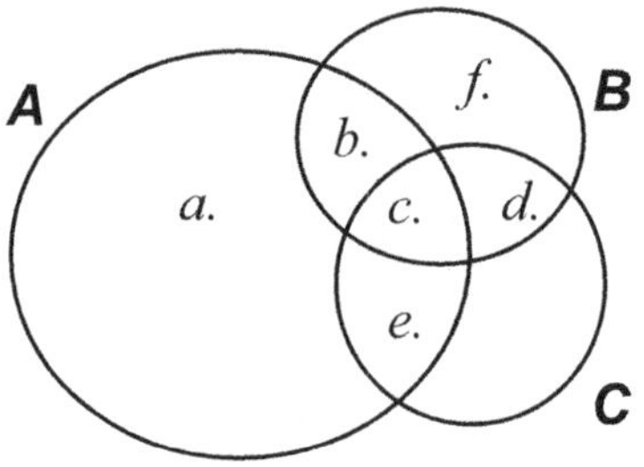

5. $\mathbf{H} \subset \mathbf{G}$ $\mathbf{F} \subset \mathbf{G}$ $\mathbf{H} \subset \mathbf{F}$

6. Correct, incorrect, incorrect, correct, incorrect, correct.

7. $\mathbf{A} \not\subseteq \mathbf{B} \Leftrightarrow \exists x \in \mathbf{A} \wedge x \notin \mathbf{B}$

8. *a)* $\mathbf{X} = \mathbf{D}$ *b)* $\mathrm{X} = \mathbf{E}$ or $\mathbf{X} = \mathbf{F}$ *c)* $\mathrm{X} = \mathbf{B}$ *d)* $\mathbf{X} = \mathbf{D}$

9. False

10. $\mathbf{L_1} = \{500\}$ $\mathbf{L_2} = \{500, 934\}$ $\mathbf{L_3} = \{500, 1000\}$

11. *a)* $\mathbf{A^c} = \{d, n, r, c\}$ $\mathbf{B^c} = \{a, d, c\}$ $\mathbf{C^c} = \varnothing$

b) $\varnothing^c$ is the given universal set.

c) It is not possible to determine because $\{1, 3, z\} \not\subseteq \mathbf{U}$

12.

$\mathbf{P(A)} = \{\varnothing, \{a\}, \{3\}, \{p\}, \{a,3\}, \{a, p\}, \{3, p\}, A\}$

$\mathbf{P(B)} = \{\varnothing, \{5\}, \{x\}, \{5, x\}\}$

$\mathbf{P(C)} = \{\varnothing, 1\}$

$\mathbf{P(D)} = \{\varnothing, \{5\}, \{6\}, \{7\}, \{8\}, \{5, 6\}, \{5, 7\}, \{5, 8\}, \{6, 7\},$
$\{6, 8\}, \{7, 8\}, \{5, 6, 7\}, \{5, 7, 8\}, \{5, 6, 8\}, \{6, 7, 8\}, D\}$

13. $\mathbf{P(B)} = \{\varnothing, \{\text{EARTH}\}, \{\text{WIND}\}, \{\text{FIRE}\}, \{\text{EARTH, WIND}\}, \{\text{EARTH, FIRE}\}, \{\text{WIND, FIRE}\}, B\}$

14. *a)* F *b)* T *c)* F *d)* T *e)* F

EXERCISES III

1.

a) $\mathbf{A} \cap \mathbf{B} = \{2, 4, 6\}$

b) $\mathbf{C} \cap \mathbf{D} = \{6, 8\}$

c) $\mathbf{E} \cap \mathbf{F} = \{1, 2, 3, 4, 5, 7\}$

3.

a) $\mathbf{A} \cup \mathbf{B} = \{1, 2, 3, 4, 5, 7\}$

b) $\mathbf{C} \cup \mathbf{D} = \{1, 5, 6, 7, 8, 9, 10, 11, 12, 13, 14, 15, 16, 17, 18, 19, 20, 25\}$

c) $\mathbf{E} \cup \mathbf{F} = \{1, 2, 3, 4, 5, 6, 8, 12\}$

d) $\mathbf{P} \cup \mathbf{Q} = \{2, 3, 4, 5, 6, 7, 8, 9\}$

e) $\mathbf{R} \cup \mathbf{S} = \{x : x \in N \wedge 1 < x \leq 7 \vee x > 10\}$

5.

$\mathbf{A} \cup \mathbf{B} = \{1, 2, 3, 4, 5\}$ $\mathbf{A} \cup \mathbf{C} = \{1, 2, 3, 4, 5\}$

$\mathbf{A} \cup \mathbf{D} = \{1, 2, 3, 4, 5, 7\}$ $\mathbf{A} \cap \mathbf{C} = \{1, 3\}$

$\mathbf{B} \cap \mathbf{A} = \{3, 4\}$ $\mathbf{B} \cup \mathbf{C} = \{1, 3, 4, 5\}$

$\mathbf{B} \cap \mathbf{C} = \{3, 5\}$ $\mathbf{B} \cup \mathbf{D} = \{1, 2, 3, 4, 5, 7\}$

$\mathbf{D} \cap \mathbf{A} = \{1, 2\}$ $\mathbf{D} \cup \mathbf{C} = \{1, 2, 3, 5, 7\}$

$\mathbf{B} \cap \mathbf{D} = \{5\}$ $\mathbf{C} \cap \mathbf{A} = \{1, 3\}$

6. $\mathbf{F} = \varnothing$ y $\mathbf{G} = \varnothing$

7. No

8. $\mathbf{F} = \varnothing$

9. *a)* $\varnothing$ *b)* $\{0\}$ *c)* $\varnothing$ *d)* **P** *e)* P
f) $\{\varnothing, 0\}$ *g)* $\varnothing$ *h)* $\{\varnothing\}$ *i)* $\varnothing$ *j)* $\varnothing$
k) U *l)* $\varnothing$ *m)* U *n)* $\varnothing$

10. $\mathbf{A} - \mathbf{B} = \{b, c\}$ $\text{C} - \mathbf{D} = \{17, 27\}$ $\mathbf{P} - \mathbf{Z} = \{\text{single female students}\}$

12. $\mathbf{A} - \mathbf{B} = \{c, d\}$ $\mathbf{B} - \mathbf{C} = \{b\}$ $\mathbf{A} \cup \mathbf{B} = \{\text{a}, b, c, d, i\}$
$\mathbf{C} - \mathbf{D} = \{a, e, i, o\}$ $\mathbf{D} - \mathbf{C} = \{f, g, c\}$ $\mathbf{C} \,\Delta\, \mathbf{D} = \{a, e, i, o, f, g, c\}$
$\mathbf{A} \,\Delta\, \mathbf{B} = \{c, d, i\}$ $\mathbf{D} - \mathbf{B} = \{f, g, c\}$ $\mathbf{C} \cap \mathbf{D} = \varnothing$
$\mathbf{A} - \mathbf{D} = \{a, b, d\}$ $\mathbf{B} \cup \mathbf{C} = \{a, b, i, e, o\}$ $\mathbf{D} \cap \mathbf{B} = \varnothing$
$\mathbf{B} \,\Delta\, \mathbf{C} = \{b, e, o\}$ $\mathbf{C} \,\Delta\, \mathbf{B} = \{b, e, o\}$ $\mathbf{D} - \mathbf{A} = \{f, g\}$

13. *a)* T *b)* T *c)* T *d)* T *e)* F
f) T *g)* T *h)* F

14. $(\mathbf{A} \cup \mathbf{B}) - \mathbf{C} = \{1, 6, 8\}$ $(\mathbf{A} \cap \mathbf{C}) - \mathbf{C} = \varnothing$
$[(\mathbf{A} \cup \mathbf{C}) \cap \mathbf{B}] - (\mathbf{A} \cup \mathbf{B}) = \varnothing$ $(\mathbf{B} \cap \mathbf{C}) - (\mathbf{A} \cup \mathbf{C}) = \varnothing$
$(\mathbf{B} \cap \mathbf{C}) - (\mathbf{B} \cup \mathbf{C}) = \varnothing$ $(\mathbf{B} \cup \mathbf{C}) - (\mathbf{B} \cap \mathbf{C}) = \{1, 2, 4, 6\}$
$\mathbf{A} \cup (\mathbf{B} - \mathbf{A}) = \{1, 2, 3, 4, 5, 6, 8\}$ $\mathbf{A} \cap (\mathbf{B} - \mathbf{A}) = \varnothing$

15. $(\mathbf{A} - \mathbf{B}) \cup \mathbf{C} = \{2, 4, 14, 16, 18\}$ $\mathbf{P(C)} = \{\varnothing, \{2\}, \{4\}, \{2, 4\}\}$

$\mathbf{C_B C} = \{1, 3, 6, 12\}$ $\mathbf{C - B} = \varnothing$

16. $(\mathbf{B} \cup \mathbf{C}) \cap \mathbf{A} = \mathbf{A}$ $\mathbf{A} \,\Delta\, \mathbf{B} = \{-3, 1, 2\}$
$(\mathbf{A} - \mathbf{B}) \cup (\mathbf{B} \cup \mathbf{C}) = \{0, 1, 2\}$

17. $\mathbf{H} - \mathbf{M} = \{1\}$ $\mathbf{P(H)} = \{\varnothing, \{1\}, \{2\}, \{4\}, \{1, 2\}, \{1, 4\}, \{2, 4\}, H\}$
$C_M J = \{6, 8, 10\}$

18. *a)* $(\mathbf{A} \cup \mathbf{B})^c$ *b)* $(\mathbf{A} \cap \mathbf{B})^c$ *c)* $\mathrm{A} - \mathbf{B}$
d) $(\mathbf{B} - \mathbf{A})^c$ *e)* $(\mathbf{A} - \mathbf{B}) \cup (\mathbf{A} \cap \mathbf{B})$ or $\mathbf{A}$
f) $(\mathbf{A} \,\Delta\, \mathbf{B})^c$ *g)* $(\mathbf{B} - \mathbf{A}) \cup (\mathbf{A} \cap \mathbf{B})$ or $\mathbf{B}$
h) $\mathbf{A}^c$ *i)* $(\mathbf{A} \cup \mathbf{B})^c$

19. *a)* F *b)* T *c)* F
d) T *e)* F *f)* T

20. *a) Necessary* and sufficient *b)* Necessary and sufficient
c) Necessary and sufficient *d)* Necessary

22. *a)* No *b)* Yes *c)* Yes *d)* No

24. $\mathbf{P(A)} = \{\varnothing, \{2\}, \{\{2, 3\}\}, \{\varnothing\}, \{2, \{2, 3\}\}, \{2, \varnothing\}, \{\{2, 3\}, \varnothing\}, \mathbf{A}\}$
$\mathbf{P(B)} = \{\varnothing, \{\{0\}\}, \{0\}, \{\{b\}\}, \{\{0\}, 0\}, \{\{0\}, \{b\}\}, \{0, \{b\}\}, \mathbf{B}\}$
$\mathbf{P(C)} = \{\varnothing, \{1\}, \{2\}, \{\{\varnothing\}\}, \{a\}, \{1, \{\varnothing\}\}, \{1, a\}, \{1, 2\}, \{2, \{\varnothing\}\}, \{2, a\}, \{\{\varnothing\}, a\}, \{1, 2, \{\varnothing\}\}, \{1, 2, a\}, \{1, \{\varnothing\}, a\}, \{2, \{\varnothing\}, a\}, C\}$

26. $n(\mathbf{A} \cup \mathbf{B} \cup \mathbf{C}) = n(\mathbf{A}) + n(\mathbf{B}) + n(\mathbf{C}) - n(\mathbf{A} \cap \mathbf{B}) + n(\mathbf{A} \cap \mathbf{C}) + n(\mathbf{B} \cap \mathbf{C}) + n(\mathbf{A} \cap \mathbf{B} \cap \mathbf{C})$

27. 120

28. It is incorrect because there are 162 students in Sciences.

29. 34

30. *a)* 190 *b)* 245 *c)* 490

31. *a)* 40 *b)* 30 *c)* 172 *d)* 340

32. *a)* Yes *b)* No *c)* No *d)* Yes

33. *a)* No *b)* Yes *c)* No *d)* Yes *e)* No

EXERCISES IV

1.

a) T	*b)* F	*c)* T	*d)* T	*e)* T
f) T	*g)* F	*h)* T	*i)* F	*j)* F
k) F	*l)* T	*m)* F	*n)* T	*o)* F
p) T	*q)* T	*r)* F	*s)* F	*t)* F

2.

A = $\{x\text{: } x \in \boldsymbol{R} \wedge -3 \leq x < 5\}$ **B** = $\{x\text{: } x \in \boldsymbol{R} \wedge 4 < x < 10\}$

C = $\{x\text{: } x \in \boldsymbol{R} \wedge 0 \leq x \leq 7\}$ **D** = $\{x\text{: } x \in \boldsymbol{R} \wedge -5 > x \leq 3\}$

E = $\{x\text{: } x \in \boldsymbol{R} \wedge -7 \leq x < -2\}$ **F** = $\{x\text{: } x \in \boldsymbol{R} \wedge 0 < x < 4\}$

G = $\{x\text{: } x \in \boldsymbol{R} \wedge -3 \leq x < -2\}$ **H** = $\{x\text{: } x \in \boldsymbol{R} \wedge -2 < x \leq 8\}$

I = $\{x\text{: } x \in \boldsymbol{R} \wedge 2 < x \leq 5\}$ **J** = $\{x\text{: } x \in \boldsymbol{R} \wedge -3 \leq x \leq 0\}$

3. **A** = $(-\infty, 3)$ **B** = $(-2, \infty)$ **C** = $[-5, \infty)$

D = $(-\infty, 7]$ **E** = $(0, 3]$ **F** = $[3, \infty)$

G = $[-3, 3)$ **H** = $[-1/2, \sqrt{2})$ **I** = $(-1, 3)$

4. *a)* $[-4, 3/2)$ *b)* $[-4, -1]$ *c)* $\varnothing$

d) $(-\infty, 3/2)$

e) $(1, 3/2)$ *f)* $(-1, 1/2)$ *g)* $[1/2, 3/2)$

h) $[-4, 1/2)$

i) $(-\infty, -4) \cup [1/2, 1]$ *j)* $(-1, 1]$

k) $(-\infty, -1]$ *l)* $[-4, -1] \cup [1/2, 3/2)$

m) $(-\infty, -4) \cup [1/2, 1]$

n) $(-\infty, -1] \cup (1, 3/2)$ *o)* $(-\infty, 1]$

5. *a)* $[-2, 2]$ *b)* $(-\infty, -3) \cup (0, \infty)$

c) $(-\infty, 0) \cup (5, \infty)$ *d)* $(7, \infty)$

e) $(-\infty, 0) \cup [5, \infty)$ *f)* $(0, 2)$

g) $(-\infty, -1) \cup (3, \infty)$ *h)* $(-\infty, -3) \cup [-2, \infty)$

i) $(2, 4)$ *j)* $[0, 3]$

6. *a)* $(1, 5/2]$ *b)* $(5/2, \infty)$ *c)* $(-\infty, -1]$ *d)* $(-\infty, -1] \cup (5/2, \infty)$
e) $(-\infty, \infty)$ *f)* $(-\infty, -1]$ *g)* $(5/2, \infty)$ *h)* $(-\infty, -1] \cup (5/2, \infty)$

7. *a)* No *b)* No *c)* No *d)* Yes *e)* No *f)* Yes

8. *a)* No *b)* Yes *c)* No *d)* No *e)* No f) No g) No
h) Yes *i)* Yes

Chapter 3: The Real Number System

In the previous chapter, we described the development of the different types of numerical sets that led to the definition of the set of real numbers. In this chapter, the definition of *the real number system* will be addressed by using an axiomatic approach. In doing this we must address concepts that in turn are essential for the development of fundamental concepts of Calculus that students of mathematics must handle properly.

The real number system is constituted by the set of real numbers, two fundamental operations: addition (+) and multiplication (· or x), and the binary relation "less than" (<) which satisfy the following axioms:

Addition

1) Closure:

$$\forall\ a, b \in \boldsymbol{R}, (a + b) \in \boldsymbol{R}$$

2) Commutative law:

$$\forall\ a, b \in \boldsymbol{R}, \mathrm{a} + b = b + a$$

3) Associative law:

$$\forall\ a, b, c \in \boldsymbol{R}, (a + b) + c = a + (b + c)$$

4) Existence and uniqueness of identity element:

$$\exists\ 0 \in \boldsymbol{R}: \forall\ a \in \boldsymbol{R}, a + 0 = 0 + a = a$$

5) Existence and uniqueness of inverse element:

$$\forall\ a \in \boldsymbol{R}, \exists\ (-a) \in \boldsymbol{R}: a + (-a) = (-a) + a = 0$$

From Axiom 5 we have that

$$\forall\ a \in \boldsymbol{R}:\ -(-a) = a$$

This means that the additive inverse of $(-a)$ is a.

The arithmetic operation known as *subtraction* is derived from the addition operation and axiom 5. In fact, given two any real numbers a and b and being $(-b)$ the additive inverse of b, we can write the difference between a and b as follows:

$$a - b = a + (-b)$$

Note that the additive identity defined in Axiom 4 is a unique element for *all* real numbers. It is denoted by "0" and read as "zero". While the additive inverse defined in Axiom 5 is unique for *each* real number. Thus, for *each* real number there is *one and only one* additive inverse. The additive inverse is also known as the *opposite* element. Then, being a any real number, $(-a)$ is the opposite of a and vice versa.

Multiplication

6) Closure:

$$\forall\ a, b \in \boldsymbol{R}, (a \cdot b) \in \boldsymbol{R}$$

7) Commutative law:

$$\forall\ a, b \in \boldsymbol{R},\ a \cdot b = b \cdot a$$

8) Associative law:

$$\forall\ a, b, c \in \boldsymbol{R},\ (a \cdot b) \cdot c = a \cdot (b \cdot c)$$

9) Existence and uniqueness of identity element:

$$\exists\ 1 \in R\colon \forall\ a \in R \wedge a \neq 0,\ a \cdot 1 = 1 \cdot a = a$$

10) Existence and uniqueness of inverse element:

$$\forall\ a \in \boldsymbol{R} \wedge a \neq 0,\ \exists\ a^{-1} \in \boldsymbol{R}\colon a \cdot a^{-1} = a^{-1} \cdot a = 1$$

From Axiom 10 we have that

$$\forall\ a \in \boldsymbol{R} \wedge a \neq 0\colon (a^{-1})^{-1} = a$$

This means that the multiplicative inverse of a^{-1} is a and vice versa.

The arithmetic operation known as *division* is derived from the multiplication operation and axiom 10. In fact, given two any real numbers a and b, being $b \neq 0$ and b^{-1} the multiplicative inverse of b, we can write the quotient a/b as

$$\frac{a}{b} = a.b^{-1}$$

If $a = 1$, then we have that

$$\frac{1}{b} = 1.b^{-1} = b^{-1}$$

Note that the multiplicative identity defined in Axiom 9 is a unique element for *all non-zero* real numbers. It is denoted by "1" and read as "one". While the multiplicative inverse defined in Axiom 10 is unique for *each non-zero* real number. This is, for *each* non-zero real number there is *one and only one* multiplicative inverse.

The following axiom establishes a connection between multiplication and addition operations:

11) Distributive law:

$$\forall\, a, b, c \in \boldsymbol{R},\ \mathrm{a} \cdot (b + c) = a \cdot b + a \cdot c = b \cdot a + c \cdot a = (b + c) \cdot a$$

Relation "less than"

12) Trichotomy:

$$\forall\, a, b \in \boldsymbol{R},\ (a < b) \vee (a = b) \vee (b < a)$$

13) Transitive law:

$$\forall\, a, b, c \in \boldsymbol{R},\ (a < b \wedge b < c) \Rightarrow \mathrm{a} < c$$

The following axioms connect the relation "less than" with the multiplication and addition operations respectively:

14) $$\forall\, a, b, c \in \boldsymbol{R},\ (a < b) \Rightarrow (a + c < b + c)$$

15) $$\forall\, a, b, c \in \boldsymbol{R} \wedge (0 < c),\ (a < b) \Rightarrow (a \cdot c < \mathrm{b} \cdot c)$$

16) Least upper bound (supremum) axiom

To formally state this axiom, it is necessary to discuss previously the concepts of bounds, maximum, and minimum of real number sets, which also play an important role in the definitions of fundamental concepts of Calculus.

BOUNDS OF SETS

Given the set A such that $A \subset \mathbf{R}$,

A is *bounded above* $\Leftrightarrow \exists\, d \in \mathbf{R}: x \leq d;\ \forall\, x \in \mathbf{A}$

The number d is called an *upper bound* of A.

Let us use the example of an open interval such as (a, b). In this case, the number b and any real number greater than b satisfy the definition of being an upper bound of the interval (a, b). This is still true even when the interval is closed.

In general, for any given set of real numbers, if there is one upper bound, then there are an infinite number of upper bounds for the same given set.

We denote the set of upper bounds of a given set A by ***UB(A)***. Thus, in the case of the open interval (a, b), the set of upper bounds is described as follows:

$$\mathbf{UB(a, b)} = \{x \in \mathbf{R}: b \leq x\} = [b, \infty)$$

This set is also the set of upper bounds for the closed interval $[a, b]$. Figure 3.1 illustrates the set ***UB(a, b) = UB[a, b]***.

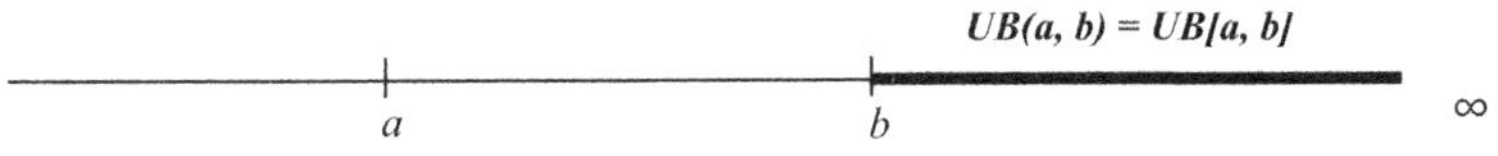

Figure 3.1

Those intervals whose upper ends are not finite such as (a, ∞), $[a, \infty)$, and $(-\infty, \infty)$ are unbounded above.

> Given the set A such that $A \subset \mathbf{R}$,
>
> **A** is *bounded below* $\Leftrightarrow \exists\, c \in \mathbf{R}: c \leq x;\ \forall\, x \in \mathbf{A}$
>
> The number c is called a *lower bound* of A.

Let us use again the example of an open interval such as (a, b). In this case, the number a and any real number less than a satisfy the definition of being a lower bound of the interval (a, b). Note that the situation is the same if the interval is closed.

In general, for any given set of real numbers, if there is one lower bound, then there are an infinite number of lower bounds for the same given set.

We denote the set of lower bounds of a given set A by ***LB(A)***. Thus, in the case of the open interval (a, b), the set of lower bounds is described as follows:

$$\mathbf{LB(a, b)} = \{x \in \boldsymbol{R}: x \leq a\} = (-\infty, a]$$

This set is also the set of lower bounds for the closed interval $[a, b]$. Figure 3.2 illustrates the set ***LB(a, b) = LB[a, b]***.

Figure 3.2

Those intervals whose lower ends are not finite such as $(-\infty, b)$, $(-\infty, b]$, and $(-\infty, \infty)$ are unbounded below.

Any set of real numbers which is both bounded above and bounded below is called *bounded.* Formally, the definition is as follows:

> Given the set A such that $A \subset R$,
>
> $\mathbf{A}$ is *bounded* $\Leftrightarrow \exists\, c, d \in R$: $c \leq x \leq d;\ \forall\, x \in \mathbf{A}$

The intervals (a, b) and $[a, b]$ are examples of bounded sets. Figure 3.3 provides an illustration.

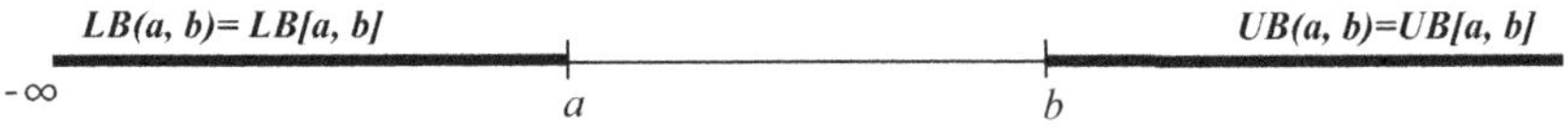

Figure 3.3

The intervals (a, ∞) and $[a, \infty)$ are both unbounded since they are unbounded above even though they are bounded below. Likewise, the intervals $(-\infty, b)$ and $(-\infty, b]$ are both unbounded because they are unbounded below even though they are bounded above.

MAXIMUM AND MINIMUN OF SETS

The *maximum* of a set of real numbers is the largest of all numbers that belong to the set, while the *minimum* is the smallest. The formal definitions are provided below.

> Given the set A such that $A \subset R$,
>
> m is the *maximum* of $\mathbf{A} \Leftrightarrow m \in \mathbf{A} \wedge x \leq m;\ \forall\, x \in \mathbf{A}$
>
> n is the *minimum* of $\mathbf{A} \Leftrightarrow n \in \mathbf{A} \wedge n \leq x;\ \forall\, x \in \mathbf{A}$

We denote the maximum of a set A by *max* A and the minimum by *min* A. Then, according to the given definitions, they are

$$m = max\ \mathbf{A} \qquad \text{and} \qquad n = min\ \mathbf{A}$$

If a set has a maximum (minimum), then it is unique. This is formally stated by the following theorem:

Theorem 1

Given the set $A \subseteq R$ and $a, b \in A$

$$(a = max\ \mathbf{A}) \wedge (b = max\ \mathbf{A}) \Rightarrow (a = b)$$

Proof:

$(a = max\ A) \wedge (b = max\ A)$

$[(a = max\ A) \wedge (b = max\ A)] \Rightarrow [(\forall\, x \in A: x \leq a) \wedge (\forall\, x \in A: x \leq b)]$ by definition

$[(\forall\, x \in A: x \leq a) \wedge (\forall\, x \in A: x \leq b)] \Rightarrow [(b \leq a) \wedge (a \leq b)]$ since $a, b \in A$

$[(b \leq a) \wedge (a \leq b)] \Rightarrow (a = b)$

$$\therefore (a = b)$$

Note that the definitions of upper bounds and maximum are similar. However, there is an important difference: if they exist, the maximum is unique, and it belongs to the given set, while upper bounds may or may not belong to the set and there are an infinite number of them.

The proof for the minimum case is like the one provided for the maximum case. Therefore, we leave this proof as an exercise for the student. In the same way, the definitions of lower bounds and minimum are similar. The difference is the same that was highlighted in the case of maximum and upper bounds.

As an illustration, let us take the case of the closed interval $[a, b]$. The elements a and b are the minimum and the maximum, respectively. However, in the case of the open interval (a, b), there is neither maximum nor minimum. The proof that this interval has no maximum is as follows:

Proof:

Let us assume that the interval (a, b) does have a maximum which is c. Then, according to the definition, we have that

$$c \in (a, b) \wedge [\forall\, x \in (a, b) \Rightarrow x \leq c]$$

Since c belongs to the interval (a, b), then

$$a < c < b$$

As we may recall, the set of real numbers satisfies the density property. Therefore, between c and b there are infinite real numbers that belong to (a, b) which are less than b and greater than c contradicting the assumption that c is the maximum. Then, the interval (a, b) does not have a maximum.

The non-existence of a minimum of (a, b) can be proven by similar reasoning.

SUPREMUM AND INFIMUM

The supremum of a given set of real numbers is the least of its upper bounds, while the infimum is the greatest of its lower bounds.

We can see the supremum (infimum) correspond with the minimum (maximum) of the set of upper (lower) bounds, respectively. The formal definitions are as follows:

Given the set $\boldsymbol{A}$ such that $\boldsymbol{A} \subset \boldsymbol{R}$ and $\boldsymbol{A}$ bounded above

$$s \text{ is the } \textit{supremum} \text{ of } \mathbf{A} \Leftrightarrow s = \textit{min}\ \mathbf{UB(A)}$$

$$i \text{ is the } \textit{infimum} \text{ of } \mathbf{A} \Leftrightarrow i = \textit{max}\ \mathbf{LB(A)}$$

We denote the supremum by *Sup* ***A*** and the infimum by *Inf* ***A*** such that, according to the given definitions, they are

$$Sup\ A = \mathrm{s} \qquad \text{and} \qquad Inf\ A = i$$

Let us illustrate these definitions by taking the case of the closed interval $[a, b]$. This interval has both a supremum and an infimum which are b and a, respectively. In this case, supremum and infimum equal the maximum and the minimum of the interval, respectively.

If we have the open interval (a, b) the supremum and the infimum are also b and a, respectively, but in this case, they do not match with the maximum and the minimum because, as we discussed it earlier, such extreme elements do not exist for this interval.

In general, we can state that given a set of real numbers $\boldsymbol{A}$, which is bounded above, if the supremum belongs to $\boldsymbol{A}$, then it equals the maximum. If the supremum does not belong to $\boldsymbol{A}$, then the set $\boldsymbol{A}$ does not have a maximum. The same conclusion applies to the infimum and the minimum.

We can now enunciate Axiom 16 properly.

Supremum axiom

$$\mathbf{A} \subset \boldsymbol{R} \wedge \mathbf{A} \neq \varnothing \wedge \mathbf{A} \text{ bounded above} \Rightarrow \exists\ Sup\ \mathbf{A} \in \boldsymbol{R}$$

Based on this axiomatic approach, it is interesting to establish the differences between the numerical sets studied in the previous chapter by observing which axioms satisfy the different numerical sets.

Thus, ***N*** satisfies axioms 1 to 4, 6 to 9, and 11 to 15. Therefore, axioms 5, 10, and 16 are not satisfied by ***N***. The extension of the numerical set to ***Z*** allows satisfying axiom 5 but axioms 10 and 16 are still not satisfied. The extension to ***Q*** allows satisfying axiom 10 but not 16. This means that not every subset of ***Q*** that is bounded above has a supremum in ***Q***. As an example, let us have the following set:

$$\mathbf{S} = \{x : x \in \boldsymbol{Q} \wedge x \geq 0 \wedge x^2 < 2\}$$

The set ***S*** is bounded above whose least upper bound must be a number c such that

$$c^2 = 2$$

This means that

$$Sup\ \mathbf{S} = c$$

However, we proved earlier that there is not any rational number whose square equals 2. Therefore, ***S*** defined as a subset of ***Q*** has a supremum which is not in ***Q***.

The extension to ***R*** constitutes a set of numbers that satisfies all sixteen axioms. In this way we can see that axiom 16 establishes the difference between ***Q*** and ***R***.

The sixteen axioms are the basic properties that *R* satisfies. Based on these axioms, other important properties can be proven. Many of these properties are already known by the students which are often taken for granted.

However, these properties in fact constitute theorems that need to be proven. We provide proof of some of them below and this also allows us to show how to apply these axioms in mathematical demonstrations.

Theorem 2

$$a \in R \Rightarrow a \,.\, 0 = 0 \,.\, a = 0$$

Proof:

$a \,.\, 0 = a \,.\, 0 + 0$	By axiom 4
$= a \,.\, 0 + [a + (-a)]$	By axiom 5
$= (a \,.\, 0 + a) + (-a)$	By axiom 3
$= (a \,.\, 0 + a \,.\, 1) + (-a)$	By axiom 9
$= a \,.\, (0 + 1) + (-a)$	By axiom 11
$= a \,.\, 1 + (-a)$	By axiom 4
$= a + (-a)$	By axiom 9
$= 0$	By axiom 5

$\therefore a \,.\, 0 = 0$

Also

$0 \,.\, a = 0$ By axiom 7 and theorem 2

Theorem 3

$$a \in R \Rightarrow -a = (-1) \,.\, a$$

We need to prove first that

$$a + (-1).\, a = 0$$

Proof:

$a + (-1).\, a = 1.\, a + (-1).\, a$	By axiom 9
$= [1 + (-1)].\, a$	By axiom 11
$= 0.\, a$	By axiom 5
$= 0$	By theorem 2

Then, according to axiom 5, the above means that (-1). *a* is the inverse element of *a* which has been denoted by –*a* and this proves this theorem.

Theorem 4

$$a \in R \wedge b \in R \Rightarrow a\ .\ (-b) = -\ (a\ .\ b) = (-a)\ .\ b$$

Proof:

$a\ .\ (-b)$	$= a\ .\ [(-1).\ b]$	By theorem 3
	$= a\ .\ [b\ .(-1)]$	By axiom 7
	$= (a\ .\ b)\ .\ (-1)$	By axiom 8
	$= (-1)\ .\ (a\ .\ b)$	By axiom 7
	$= -\ (a\ .\ b)$	By theorem 3

$\therefore$ a . $(-b) = -\ (a\ .\ b)$

We leave the proof of $(-a)\ .\ b = -\ (a\ .\ b)$ as an exercise for the students. This proof is analogous to the previous one.

Corollary

$$a \in R \wedge b \in R \Rightarrow (-a)\ .\ (-b) = a\ .\ b$$

Proof:

$(-a)\ .\ (-b)$	$= -[a\ .\ (-b)]$	By theorem 4
	$= -[-(a\ .\ b)]$	By theorem 4
	$= a\ .\ b$	By axiom 5

$\therefore (-a)\ .\ (-b) \quad = a\ .\ b$

To complete this axiomatic definition of real numbers, we must highlight the fact that the division by the real number zero is not defined.

The real number zero does not satisfy axiom 10 which refers the existence of a multiplicative inverse. If there is such an inverse element for zero, this fact would produce a contradiction against the rest of the axioms. Let us look at this issue more closely.

Let us suppose that there is a multiplicative inverse for the real number zero which we assume is *c*. If this is true, according to the axiom 10, it must be satisfied that

$$0 \, . \, c = 1$$

However, this result contradicts Theorem 2. Since we derived the division of real numbers from axiom 10, we conclude that the division by zero cannot be defined.

EXERCISES I

Given the real numbers *a, b*, and *c*, prove the following properties:

1. $- a - b = - (a + b)$
2. $a + b = a + c \Rightarrow b = c$ (Additive cancellation property)
3. $-0 = 0$
4. $a \, . \, b = 0 \Rightarrow a = 0 \vee b = 0$
5. $1^{-1} = 1$
6. $a \, . \, b = a \, . \, c \wedge a \neq 0 \Rightarrow b = c$
   (Multiplicative cancellation property)

INEQUELITIES

In this section we focus our attention on another set of properties (theorems) that involve the relation "less than". We will consider only some of them. The corresponding demonstrations are supported by the axioms and properties previously proven. Let us assume that *a, b,* and *c* are any real numbers.

Theorem 5

$$a < b \wedge c < d \Rightarrow a + c < b + d$$

Proof:

$a < b \wedge c < d$	
$a < b \wedge c < d \Rightarrow (a + c < b + c) \wedge (b + c < b + d)$	By axiom 14
$\Rightarrow a + c < b + d$	By axiom 13
$\therefore a + c < b + d$	

Theorem 6

$$a < b \Rightarrow -b < -a$$

Proof:

$a < b$	
$a < b \Rightarrow a + (-a) < b + (-a)$	By axiom 14
$\Rightarrow 0 < b + (-a)$	By axiom 5
$\Rightarrow (-b) + 0 < (-b) + [b + (-a)]$	By axioms 14
$\Rightarrow -b < [(-b) + b] + (-a)$	By axioms 4 and 3
$\Rightarrow -b < 0 + (-a)$	By axiom 5
$\Rightarrow -b < -a$	By axiom 4
$\therefore -b < -a$	

Theorem 7

$$a < b \wedge c < 0 \Rightarrow b \cdot c < a \cdot c$$

Proof:

$a < b \wedge c < 0$

$a < b \wedge c < 0 \Rightarrow a < b \wedge 0 < -c$	By theorem 6 and property 3 in EXERCISES I
$\Rightarrow a.\,(-c) < b.\,(-c)$	By axiom 15
$\Rightarrow -a\,.\,c < -\,b.\,c$	By theorem 4
$\Rightarrow -\,(-\,b.\,c) < -\,(-\,a\,.\,c)$	By theorem 6
$\Rightarrow b.\,c < a\,.\,c$	By axiom 5

$\therefore b.\,c < a\,.\,c$

Theorem 8

$$a \neq 0 \Rightarrow 0 < a^2$$

Proof:

There are two cases: $a < 0$ and $0 < a$. Let us consider the first one:

$a < 0$

$a < 0 \Rightarrow 0.\,a < a\,.\,a$	By theorem 7
$\Rightarrow 0 < a^2$	By theorem 2

$\therefore 0 < a^2$

Now let us see the second case:

$0 < a$

$0 < a \Rightarrow 0\,.\,a < a\,.\,a$	By axiom 15
$\Rightarrow 0 < a^2$	By theorem 2

$\therefore 0 < a^2$

Theorem 9

$$(0 \leq a < b) \wedge (0 \leq c < d) \Rightarrow a\,.\,c < b\,.\,d$$

Proof:

$(0 \leq a < b) \wedge (0 \leq c < d)$	
$(0 \leq a < b) \wedge (0 \leq c < d) \Rightarrow 0 < b \wedge c < d$	By hypothesis
$\Rightarrow b\,.\,c < b\,.\,d$	By axiom 15
$\therefore b\,.\,c < b\,.\,d$	**(1)**

Also, we have

$(0 \leq a < b) \wedge (0 \leq c < d)$	
$(0 \leq a < b) \wedge (0 \leq c < d) \Rightarrow a < b \wedge 0 \leq c$	By hypothesis
$\Rightarrow a < b \wedge (0 < c \vee 0 = c)$	
$\Rightarrow (a < b \wedge 0 < c) \vee (a < b \wedge 0 = c)$	Distributive law
$\Rightarrow (a\,.\,c < b\,.\,c) \vee (a\,.\,c = 0 = b\,.\,c)$	By axiom 15 and theorem 2
$\therefore (a\,.\,c < b\,.\,c) \vee (a\,.\,c = 0 = b\,.\,c)$	**(2)**

From conclusions **(2)** and **(1)** and by axiom13, we get the conclusion:

$$a\,.\,c < b\,.\,d$$

Therefore, we have proven that

$$(0 \leq a < b) \wedge (0 \leq c < d) \Rightarrow a\,.\,c < b\,.d$$

Theorem 10

Being $0 \leq a$ and $0 \leq b$, we have that

$$a < b \Leftrightarrow a^2 < b^2$$

Proof:

$a < b$

$a < b \Rightarrow a\,.\,a < a\,.\,b$ By axiom 15

$\Rightarrow a^2 < a\,.\,b$

$\therefore a^2 < a\,.\,b$ **(3)**

Also

$a < b$

$a < b \Rightarrow a\,.\,b < b\,.\,b$ By axiom 15

$\Rightarrow a\,.\,b < b^2$

$\therefore a\,.\,b < b^2$ **(4)**

From conclusions **(3)** and **(4)** and by axiom13, we get the conclusion:

$$a^2 < b^2$$

Therefore, we have proven that

$$a < b \Rightarrow a^2 < b^2$$

Let us now consider the converse form. This is

$$a^2 < b^2 \Rightarrow a < b$$

In this case, we apply the indirect proof method. This means that we must prove the contrapositive form. This is:

$$\sim (a < b) \Rightarrow \sim (a^2 < b^2)$$

Or the equivalent form

$$b \leq a \Rightarrow b^2 \leq a^2$$

Then

$b \leq a$

$b \leq a \Rightarrow b\,.\,b \leq a\,.\,b$ By axiom 15

$\Rightarrow b^2 \leq a\,.\,b$

$\therefore b^2 \leq a\,.\,b$ **(5)**

Also

$b \leq a$

$b \leq a \Rightarrow a\,.\,b \leq a\,.\,a$ By axiom 15

$\Rightarrow a\,.\,b \leq a^2$

$\therefore a\,.\,b \leq a^2$ **(6)**

Like the previous cases, from conclusions **(5)** and **(6)** and by axiom13, we get the conclusion:

$$b \leq a \Rightarrow b^2 \leq a^2$$

This completes the proof of this theorem.

Theorem 11

Being $0 \leq b$ we have that

$$b < a^2 \Leftrightarrow \sqrt{b} < a \wedge a < -\sqrt{b}$$

Proof:

There are two cases: $0 \leq a$ and $a < 0$. Let us see the first one:

$b < a^2$

$b < a^2 \Leftrightarrow (\sqrt{b}\,)^2 < a^2$

$\Leftrightarrow \sqrt{b} < a$ By theorem 10

$\therefore \sqrt{b} < a$

Now, let us consider the second case ($a < 0$):

$b < a^2$	
$b < a^2 \Leftrightarrow b < (-a)^2$	Because $a < 0 \Rightarrow 0 < -a$
$\Leftrightarrow (\sqrt{b}\,)^2 < (-a)^2$	
$\Leftrightarrow \sqrt{b} < -a$	By theorem 10
$\Leftrightarrow a < -\sqrt{b}$	By theorem 6
$\therefore a < -\sqrt{b}$	

Thus, we have proven that

$$b < a^2 \Leftrightarrow \sqrt{b} < a \wedge a < -\sqrt{b}$$

EXERCISES II

1. Assume that $a, b \in \boldsymbol{R} \wedge b \geq 0$. Prove that

$$a^2 < b \Leftrightarrow -\sqrt{b} < a < \sqrt{b}$$

Hint: The proof is like the one applied to prove theorem 11.

2. Given $a, b \in \boldsymbol{R}$. Prove the following:

$$(a > 0 \wedge b > 0) \vee (a < 0 \wedge b < 0) \Leftrightarrow a \,.\, b > 0$$

and

$$(a > 0 \wedge b < 0) \vee (a < 0 \wedge b > 0) \Leftrightarrow a \,.\, b < 0$$

This is the rule of signs for multiplication.

3. Given $a \in \boldsymbol{R}$. Prove the following:

$$a > 0 \Leftrightarrow a^{-1} > 0$$

$$a < 0 \Leftrightarrow a^{-1} < 0$$

4. Given $a, b \in \boldsymbol{R}$. Prove the following:

$$a > 0 \wedge b > 0 \wedge a < b \Rightarrow b^{-1} < a^{-1}$$

$$a < 0 \wedge b < 0 \wedge a < b \Rightarrow b^{-1} < a^{-1}$$

Summary of properties

$(a, b, c \in \boldsymbol{R})$

$$\boldsymbol{a < b \wedge c < d \Rightarrow a + c < b + d}$$

$$\boldsymbol{a < b \Rightarrow -b < -a}$$

$$\boldsymbol{a < b \wedge c < 0 \Rightarrow b \,.\, c < a \,.\, c}$$

$$\boldsymbol{a \neq 0 \Rightarrow 0 < a^2}$$

$$\boldsymbol{(0 \leq a < b) \wedge (0 \leq c < d) \Rightarrow a \,.\, c < b \,.\, d}$$

$$\boldsymbol{a < b \Leftrightarrow a^2 < b^2;\ 0 \leq a \wedge 0 \leq b}$$

$$\boldsymbol{b < a^2 \Leftrightarrow \sqrt{b} < a \wedge a < -\sqrt{b}\ ;\ 0 \leq b}$$

$$\boldsymbol{a^2 < b \Leftrightarrow -\sqrt{b} < a < \sqrt{b}\ ;\ 0 \leq b}$$

$$\boldsymbol{(a > 0 \wedge b > 0) \vee (a < 0 \wedge b < 0) \Leftrightarrow a \,.\, b > 0}$$

$$\boldsymbol{(a > 0 \wedge b < 0) \vee (a < 0 \wedge b > 0) \Leftrightarrow a \,.\, b < 0}$$

$$\boldsymbol{a > 0 \Leftrightarrow a^{-1} > 0}$$

$$\boldsymbol{a < 0 \Leftrightarrow a^{-1} < 0}$$

$$\boldsymbol{(a > 0 \wedge b > 0) \wedge a < b \Rightarrow b^{-1} < a^{-1}}$$

$$\boldsymbol{(a < 0 \wedge b < 0) \wedge a < b \Rightarrow b^{-1} < a^{-1}}$$

Solving inequalities

The axioms that refer to the relation "less than" along with the theorems, including the ones proposed as exercises, that we studied previously, constitute a set of properties that are frequently applied when solving inequalities. The previous table provides us with a summary of these properties. The following examples show how to apply these properties to solve inequalities.

Example 1

Find the set of values of x that satisfy the following linear inequality:

$$5x - 7 < x + 1$$

Solution:

$$5x - 7 < x + 1 \Leftrightarrow 5x - 7 - x + 7 < x + 1 - x + 7 \qquad \text{By axiom 14}$$

$$\Leftrightarrow 4x < 8$$

$$\Leftrightarrow \frac{1}{4}(4x) < \frac{1}{4} \,.\, 8 \qquad \text{By axiom 15}$$

$$\Leftrightarrow x < 2$$

Then, the solution in interval notation is $(-\infty, 2)$.

Example 2

Find the set of values of x that satisfy the following quadratic inequality:

$$x^2 - 5x + 6 > 0$$

Solution:

$$x^2 - 5x + 6 > 0 \Leftrightarrow (x - 3)\,(x + 2) > 0 \qquad \text{Factoring}$$

$\Leftrightarrow [(x-3) > 0 \wedge (x+2) > 0] \vee [(x-3) < 0 \wedge (x+2) < 0]$
By property 2 in EXERCISES II

$\Leftrightarrow (x > 3 \wedge x > -2) \vee (x < 3 \wedge x < -2)$ By axiom 14

$\Leftrightarrow x > 3 \vee x < -2$ By definition of intersection

Then, the solution in interval notation is $(-\infty, -2) \cup (3, \infty)$.

Example 3

Determine the set of values of x that satisfy the following inequality:

$$2x^2 - x - 10 < 0$$

Solution:

$2x^2 - x - 10 < 0 \Leftrightarrow \frac{1}{2} . (2x^2 - x - 10) < \frac{1}{2} . 0$ By axiom 15

$\Leftrightarrow x^2 - \frac{1}{2} x - 5 < 0$ By theorem 2

$\Leftrightarrow (x - \frac{5}{2})(x + 2) < 0$ Factoring

$\Leftrightarrow [(x - \frac{5}{2}) < 0 \wedge (x+2) > 0] \vee [(x - \frac{5}{2}) > 0 \wedge (x+2) < 0]$
By property 2 in EXERCISES II

$\Leftrightarrow (x < \frac{5}{2} \wedge x > -2) \vee (x > \frac{5}{2} \wedge x < -2)$ By axiom 14

$\Leftrightarrow x < \frac{5}{2} \wedge x > -2$ By definition of intersection

Then, the solution in interval notation is (-2, 5/2). Notice that the solution $(x > 5/2) \wedge (x < -2)$ constitutes an empty set.

EXERCISES III

1. Solve the following linear inequalities:

a) $x + 5 > 2$ *b)* $3x \leq 5$ *c)* $4x + 1 < 2x + 3$

d) $3x - 3 > 7x + 12$ *e)* $-3x + 1 < 2x + 5$ *f)* $11x - 7 \leq 4x + 2$

2. Solve the following quadratic inequalities:

a) $x^2 - 5x + 6 < 0$ *b)* $x^2 - 3x - 4 > 0$

c) $2x^2 - x - 10 > 0$ *d)* $2x^2 - 3x + 4 < -x^2 + 4x$

e) $3x^2 - 7x + 6 \leq 0$ *f)* $x^2 - 4x + 5 \geq 0$

3. Determine the x values for which the statements given below are:

(1) Equal to zero (2) Less than zero (3) Grater than zero

a) $x^2 - 5x - 6$ *b)* $x^2 - 10x + 33$ *c)* $x^2 - 6x$

d) $x(x - 1)$ *e)* $x^2 + 3x + 2$ *f)* $(x^2 - 1)(x + 4)$

ABSOLUTE VALUE

$\forall x \in \boldsymbol{R}$, the *absolute value* of x is denoted by $|x|$ and defined as follows:

$$|x| = \begin{cases} -x & \text{if } x < 0 \\ x & \text{if } x \geq 0 \end{cases}$$

The concept of the absolute value of a real number plays an important role in the definition and applications of fundamental concepts of calculus that students must learn properly. The formal definition is presented above.

From the definition we can see that the absolute value of a real number is always positive except when $x = 0$. The followings are examples:

$|2| = 2$ $\quad$ $|-2| = -(-2) = 2$ $\quad$ $|0.035| = 0.035$ $\quad$ $|5/4| = 5/4$

In essence, the absolute value is a magnitude and geometrically it represents the distance from the origin to the point associated with the real number x on the number line. The concept is illustrated in Figure 3.4.

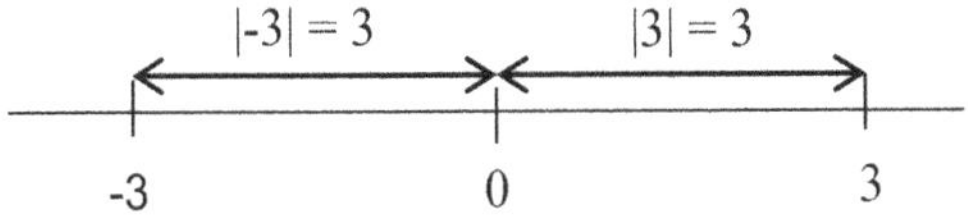

Figure 3.4

The absolute value satisfies a set of properties that are useful when solving math problems or when doing demonstrations in which this concept is involved. Some of them are presented below.

Let us assume that a and b are any real numbers. Then, they satisfy the following properties:

1) $|a| \geq 0$
2) $|a| = |-a|$
3) $|a| \geq a \wedge |a| \geq -a$
4) $|a \,.\, b| = |a| \,.\, |b|$
5) $|a + b| \leq |a| + |b|$
6) $|a - b| \geq |a| - |b|$

The first three properties are direct consequence of the definition. Therefore, we will focus our attention on the fourth and fifth properties in the following theorems while the sixth property is a corollary of the fifth.

Theorem 12

$$\forall \ a, b \in R, \ |a \, . \, b| = |a| \, . \, |b|$$

Proof:

We have two possible situations:

1) a and b are both of the same sign

2) a and b are of different sign

Let us see the first case.

1. Same sign

a) Both are positive or equal to zero

$a \geq 0 \wedge b \geq 0$

$|a| \, . \, |b| = a \, . \, b$ By definition and because $a \geq 0 \wedge b \geq 0$

$= |a \, . \, b|$ Because $a \, . \, b \geq 0$ according to the rule of signs and theorem 2

b) Both are negative

$a < 0 \wedge b < 0$

$|a \, . \, b| = |(-a). \, (-b)|$ By the corollary of theorem 4

$= |-a|. \, |-b|$ By the previous case because $-a > 0 \wedge - b > 0$

$= |a|. \, |b|$ By property 2) of absolute value

2. Different sign

Let us see the case $a \geq 0 \wedge b < 0$

$\|a \,.\, b\| = \|-(a.\, b)\|$	By property 2) of absolute value
$= \|a.\, (-b)\|$	By theorem 4
$= \|a\|.\, \|-b\|$	By the first case of a)
$= \|a\|.\, \|b\|$	By property 2) of absolute value

$\therefore\ |a \,.\, b| = |a| \,.\, |b|$

The proof of the case $a < 0 \wedge b \geq 0$ is the same as the previous demonstration just by simply exchanging the signs for a and b.

<u>Theorem 13</u>

$$\forall\ a, b \in R,\ |a + b| \leq |a| + |b|$$

Proof:

$\|a + b\|\|a + b\| = \|(a + b)(a + b)\|$	By theorem 12
$\|a + b\|^2 = \|(a + b)^2\|$	
$= (a + b)^2$	By definition
$= a^2 + 2ab + b^2$	
$\leq a^2 + 2\|a\|\|b\| + b^2$	By property 3) of absolute value
$\leq \|a\|^2 + 2\|a\|\|b\| + \|b\|^2$	By definition and theorem 12
$\leq (\|a\| + \|b\|)^2$	

$\therefore\ |a + b|^2 \leq (|a| + |b|)^2$

Therefore, based on theorem 10, we conclude that

$$|a + b| \leq |a| + |b|$$

Corollary

$$\forall\ a, b \in R,\ |a - b| \geq |a| - |b|$$

Proof:

$a = a + 0$	By axiom 4
$a = a + (-b + b)$	By axiom 5
$a = (a - b) + b$	By axiom 3
$\lvert a\rvert = \lvert (a - b) + b\rvert$	
$\lvert a\rvert \leq \lvert a - b\rvert + \lvert b\rvert$	By theorem 13
$\lvert a\rvert - \lvert b\rvert \leq \lvert a - b\rvert + \lvert b\rvert - \lvert b\rvert$	By axiom 14
$\lvert a\rvert - \lvert b\rvert \leq \lvert a - b\rvert$	By axioms 5 and 4

$$\therefore |a - b| \geq |a| - |b|$$

Solving equations and inequalities containing absolute values

Let us see some examples of applications.

Example 1

Determine the values of x that satisfy the following equation:

$$|2x + 1| = 5$$

Solution:

According to property 2 of absolute value, we have that

$$|2x + 1| = 5 \Leftrightarrow (2x + 1 = 5) \vee [\ (2x + 1) = -5)$$

$$\Leftrightarrow 2x = 4 \vee 2x = -6$$

$$\Leftrightarrow x = 2 \vee x = -3$$

Example 2

Solve the following equation:

$$|3x - 4| = x + 1$$

Solution:

In this case the possible solutions to this equation are subject to the condition $x + 1 \geq 0$, this is $x \geq -1$, because the absolute value is always greater than or equal to zero. Thus,

$$|3x - 4| = x + 1 \Leftrightarrow 3x - 4 = x + 1 \vee 3x - 4 = -(x + 1)$$

$$\Leftrightarrow 2x = 5 \vee 4x = 3$$

$$\Leftrightarrow x = 5/2 \vee x = 3/4$$

Both values are solutions of the given equation since they both satisfy the condition $x \geq -1$.

Example 3

Given that $a \in R$ and $a > 0$, determine the set of values of x that satisfy the following inequality:

$$|x| < a$$

Solution:

It was stated earlier that the absolute value of a real number x geometrically represents the distance from the origin to the point associated with the real number x on the number line. Therefore, the solution of the given inequality is the set of real numbers whose associated points on the number line lie a distance from the origin less than *a units*. This is the set of real numbers greater than $-a$ and less than a. In other words, the set of real numbers between $-a$ and a. This set is illustrated in Figure 3.5

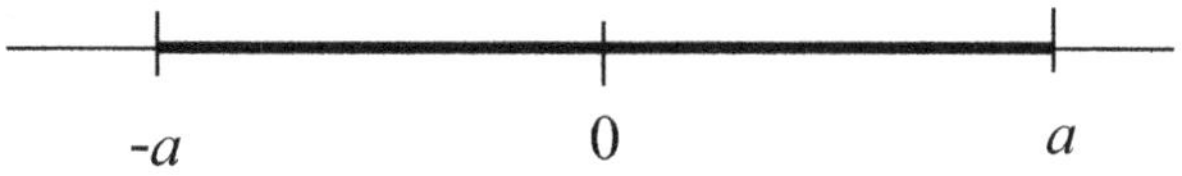

Figure 3.5

Then

$$|x| < a \Leftrightarrow x > -a \wedge x < a$$

$$\Leftrightarrow x \in (-a, a)$$

If the given inequality is stated as

$$|x| \leq a$$

Then, the solution would be the closed interval $[-a, a]$. By summarizing these results, we have:

> Given $a \in \boldsymbol{R} \wedge a > 0$,
>
> $$|x| < a \Leftrightarrow x \in (-a, a)$$
>
> $$|x| \leq a \Leftrightarrow x \in [-a, a]$$

Example 4

Given that $a \in \boldsymbol{R}$ and $a \geq 0$, determine the set of values of x that satisfy the following inequality:

$$|x| \geq a$$

<u>Solution</u>:

By following the same reasoning as in the previous example, in this case the solution is the set of real numbers that are either less than $-a$ or greater than a, because these are the numbers which are associated with points on the number line that lie a distance from the origin greater than *a units*. This set is illustrated in Figure 3.6.

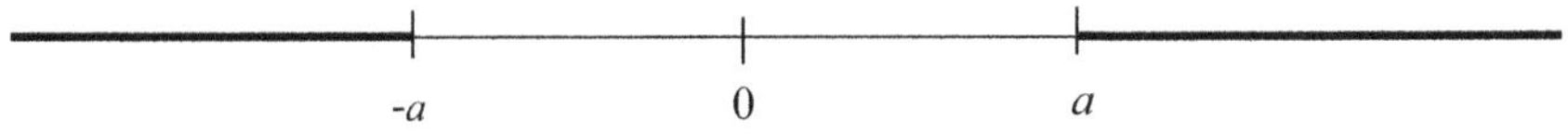

Figure 3.6

Then

$$|x| > a \Leftrightarrow x < -a \vee x > a$$

$$\Leftrightarrow x \in (-\infty, -a) \cup (a, \infty)$$

If the given inequality is stated as

$$|x| \geq a$$

Then, the solution includes both $-a$ and a. By summarizing these results, we have:

Given $a \in R \wedge a \geq 0$,

$$|x| > a \Leftrightarrow x \in (-\infty, -a) \cup (a, \infty)$$

$$|x| \geq a \Leftrightarrow x \in (-\infty, -a] \cup [a, \infty)$$

The results from examples 3 and 4 are helpful when solving inequalities that contain absolute values. Let us see some examples.

Example 5

Solve the following inequality:

$$|x - 3| < 4$$

Solution:

By applying the result from example 3 we have:

$$|x - 3| < 4 \Leftrightarrow (x - 3) > -4 \wedge (x - 3) < 4$$

$$\Leftrightarrow x > -1 \wedge x < 7$$

$$\Leftrightarrow x \in (-1, 7)$$

Example 6

Solve the following inequality:

$$|3x - 1| \geq 2x + 5$$

Solution:

In this case we apply the result from example 4.

$$|3x - 1| \geq 2x + 5 \Leftrightarrow (3x - 1) \leq -(2x + 5) \vee (3x - 1) \geq 2x + 5$$

$$\Leftrightarrow 5x \leq -4 \vee x \geq 6$$

$$\Leftrightarrow x \leq -4/5 \vee x \geq 6$$

$$\Leftrightarrow x \in (-\infty, -4/5] \cup [6, \infty)$$

It is not necessary to establish the condition $2x + 5 \geq 0$ because the values of x that make $2x + 5 < 0$ are included in the solution of the given inequality.

NEIGHBOURHOOD

As the title suggests, this concept refers to the set of real numbers that are "close" to a certain number. This set constitutes an interval, and its definition involves the concept of absolute value.

The neighbourhood of a number plays an important role in the definition of fundamental concepts of Calculus such as limit. The formal definition is as follows:

> Given the real numbers a and r such that $r > 0$,
>
> The *neighbourhood* of centre a and radius r is the set denoted by ***N(a, r)*** such that
>
> $$\mathbf{N}(\boldsymbol{a}, \boldsymbol{r}) = \{x : x \in \boldsymbol{R} \wedge |x - a| < r\}$$

According to this definition and after applying the results that we got from previous examples of inequalities that contain absolute value, we can write that

$$\mathbf{N}(\boldsymbol{a}, \boldsymbol{r}) = (a - r, a + r)$$

This means that the neighbourhood of centre a and radius r is an open interval whose endpoints are $a - r$ and $a + r$ respectively, being a the middle point of the interval. Figure 3.7 provides an illustration.

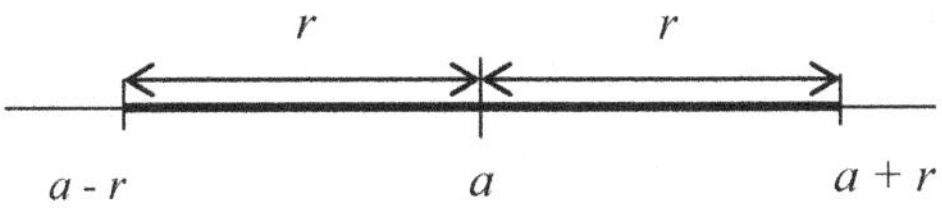

Figure 3.7

Example 8

Build a neighbourhood of centre 3 and radius 2.

<u>Solution</u>:

According to the definition, the neighbourhood of centre 3 and radius 2 is the following set:

$$\mathbf{N(3,2)} = \{x: x \in \boldsymbol{R} \wedge |x - 3| < 2\}$$
$$= (3 - 2, 3 + 2)$$
$$= (1, 5)$$

Reduced and complete neighbourhoods

The given definition of neighbourhood includes the centre and excludes the endpoints. However, the definition of some concepts of Calculus requires excluding the centre while others require including the endpoints. When the centre is excluded, the neighbourhood is known as *reduced* and it is denoted by $\boldsymbol{N^*(a, r)}$ such that

$$\mathbf{N}^*(\boldsymbol{a}, \boldsymbol{r}) = \{x: x \in \boldsymbol{R} \wedge 0 < |x - a| < r\}$$

$$= (a - r, a) \cup (a, a + r)$$

When the endpoints are included, the neighbourhood is known as *complete* and it is denoted by $\underline{\boldsymbol{N}}\boldsymbol{(a, r)}$ such that

$$\underline{N}(a, r) = \{x: x \in \boldsymbol{R} \wedge |x - a| \leq r\}$$

$$= [a - r, a + r]$$

Figure 3.8 provides illustrations.

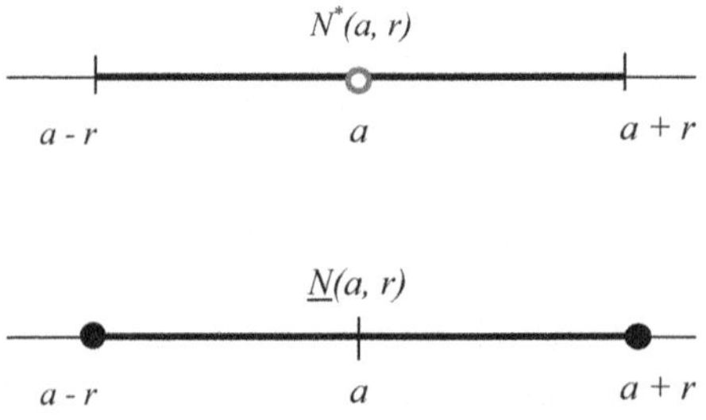

Figure 3.8

EXERCISES IV

1. Solve the following equations:

a) $|3x - 1| = 2x + 5$ *b)* $|x + 1| = 3x - 9$ *c)* $|x + 3| = |2x + 1|$

d) $|2x + 3| = x + 3$ *e)* $|x^2 + 2| = 2x + 1$ *f)* $|3x - 5| + x - 7 = 0$

2. Solve the following inequalities:

a) $|x + 3| > 7$ *b)* $|2x + 5| > 3$ *c)* $|3 + 2x| \leq 2$

d) $|3x - 1| < 4$ *e)* $|x - 2| \leq 2x$ *f)* $|2x + 1| \geq 2 + x$

3. Determine the following sets:

a) Real numbers close to -1 at a distance less than 2.

b) Real numbers close to -1 at a distance no greater than 2.

c) Real numbers close to but not equal to -1 at a distance less than 2.

d) Real numbers close to but not equal to a at a distance less than δ, being a, $\delta \in R$ and $\delta > 0$.

e) Real numbers close to but not equal to L at a distance less than ε, being L, $\varepsilon \in R$ and $\varepsilon > 0$.

ANSWERS TO THE EXERCISES PROPOSED IN CHAPTER 3

EXERCISES III

1. *a)* $x > -3$ *b)* $x \leq 5/3$ *c)* $x < 1$ *d)* $x < -15/4$

   e) $x > -4/5$ *f)* $x \leq 9/7$

2. *a)* $2 < x < 3$ *b)* $x < -1$ or $x > 4$ *c)* $x < -2$ or $x > 5/2$

   d) $1 < x < 4/3$ *e)* No solution in ***R*** *f)* ***R***

3. *a)* (1) $x = -1$ and $x = 6$ (2) $-1 < x < 6$ (3) $x < -1$ or $x > 6$

   b) It is always greater than zero for all real numbers

   c) (1) $x = 0$ and $x = 6$ (2) $0 < x < 6$ (3) $x < 0$ or $x > 6$

   d) (1) $x = 0$ and $x = 1$ (2) $0 < x < 1$ (3) $x < 0$ or $x > 1$

   e) (1) $x = -2$ and $x = -1$ (2) $-2 < x < -1$ (3) $x < -2$ or $x > -1$

   f) (1) $x = -4$, $x = -1$ and $x = 1$ (2) $x < -4$ or $-1 < x < 1$
   (3) $-4 < x < -1$ or $x > 1$

EXERCISES IV

1. *a)* $x = 6$ and $x = -4/5$ *b)* $x = 5$ *c)* $x = 2$ and $x = -4/3$

   d) $x = 0$ and $x = -2$ *e)* $x = 1$ *f)* $x = 3$ and $x = -1$

2. *a)* $x < -10$ or $x > 4$ *b)* $x < -4$ or $x > -1$ *c)* $-5/2 \leq x \leq -1/2$

   d) $-1 < x < 5/3$ *e)* $x \geq 2/3$ *f)* $x \leq -1$ or $x \geq 1$

3. *a)* $\mathbf{N(-1, 2)} = (-3, 1)$ *b)* $\mathbf{\underline{N}(-1, 2)} = [-3, 1]$

   c) $\mathbf{N^*(-1, 2)} = (-3, -1) \cup (-1, 1)$ *d)* $\mathbf{N^*(a, \delta)} = (a - \delta, a) \cup (a, a + \delta)$

   e) $\mathbf{N(L, \varepsilon)} = (L - \varepsilon, L + \varepsilon)$

Made in the USA
Coppell, TX
20 March 2021

51887127R00134